THE GATHERING OF THE FORCES OF LIGHT

UFOs and their Spiritual Mission

BENJAMIN CREME

Share International Foundation
Amsterdam • London

Manufactured in the United States on recycled paper

First Edition, July 2010

*The cover photograph is reproduced from a painting by Benjamin Creme entitled **Pluto routed** (2003).*

This book is dedicated to the memory
of a very brave man and colleague,
George Adamski (1891-1965).

CONTENTS

PHOTO PAGES

PART TWO

EDUCATION IN THE NEW AGE

PREFACE

For centuries, governments have been known to have kept much information (usually embarrassing) from their peoples, thereby consolidating their power to rule. Nevertheless, is it not surprising that for over 60 years, modern governments, aided and abetted by a cynical media, have, more or less successfully, kept from the public their certain knowledge of the reality of UFOs and the fact of their peaceful activity? Moreover, some governments have been guilty of denigrating the inhabitants of these 'non-existent' craft, have named them 'aliens', and accused them of all manner of atrocities against men and women of Earth. The reasons for this dishonest and undemocratic behaviour are discussed in this book, and the close collaboration existing between the 'people of the UFOs' (our Space Brothers) and the members of our own Spiritual Hierarchy is made clear for the first time.

The book is in two parts: the first, 'UFOs and their Spiritual Mission', deals with the work of our Space Brothers on behalf of humanity; the second, 'Education in the New Age', looks at the changes in education that will be necessary in the coming time, as we adopt new technologies introduced by the Space Brothers and become increasingly aware of the hitherto hidden forces that underlie our lives.

Part One: UFOs and their Spiritual Mission

The spiritual mission of the UFOs is made plain for all to see: our Space Brothers' constant battle on our behalf against the effects of our pollution of the planet, especially that resulting from the higher (etheric) levels of radioactivity, as yet unknown to our scientists; and the setting-up of the beginnings of our science of the future, the Science of Light. In all of this selfless service to humanity, the Space Brothers have been engaged in preparing a platform for the World Teacher, the Lord Maitreya, and in setting up the landmarks of the coming new civilization.

On 12 December 2008, Share International Foundation released through the world's media the information that a "star-like luminary of brilliant power" would very soon be visible worldwide. True to the prediction, the first reports of the 'star' started to come in at Christmas-time, and from all around the world. We related it to the biblical 'star' that led the three wise men (Masters of Wisdom) from the East to Bethlehem at the birth of Jesus. We explained that both the modern 'star' and that of two thousand years ago were in fact spacecraft, the modern 'star' being one of four such spacecraft covering the world, north, south, east and west; and that the 'star' was a Sign, a Herald of the imminent appearance on television, as yet undeclared, of Maitreya, the World Teacher, and head of our planetary Spiritual Hierarchy. These four 'stars' are gigantic spacecraft and come from the planets of our Solar System.

Our scientists assert that human life does not exist on such planets as Mars, Venus, Jupiter, etc. This assumption arises out of their ignorance of the etheric levels of matter. Their technology is still inadequate to measure the full range of the material planes. Had they etheric vision, they would know that all the planets of our system are inhabited and that many are far more advanced in evolution than we are on Earth. The time is fast approaching when a more open-minded view of life with its mysteries will supersede the arrogance of the ignorant, to the benefit of us all.

Part Two: Education in the New Age

It is obvious that an enormous educational programme will be necessary to prepare humanity for the changes inherent in the new society that will emerge under the influence of the Masters and our Space Brothers. So much that is new will be imparted that the need for interpretation will become urgent. There are many people, well informed and articulate, who can find therein a most useful field of service.

It is clear that education for the new age must be very different in purpose from that of today. The new education will seek to do more than prepare people to earn a living, as is often the case today. Instead, it will awaken humanity at the level of the soul, the source of all creativity.

From that will flow a creative vitality which will be manifested by hitherto millions of voiceless people around the world. The energy of Aquarius, that of Synthesis, will draw humanity together into a unity undreamt of today.

This, my latest book, is as always the result of group effort. I would like to gratefully acknowledge the many people who have helped to put it together and prepare it for publication.

Benjamin Creme
London, April 2010

[Note: The articles, interviews and questions and answers contained in this book were originally published in *Share International* magazine. For ease of reading the questions are arranged according to subject rather than by date of publication, which is given at the end of each question.]

PART ONE

UFOs and Their Spiritual Mission

The Time of Revelation

by the Master —, through Benjamin Creme

For many years, the peoples of most countries have followed, more or less meekly, the edicts of their legislators, the politicians. This has largely been the case whether the legislative system was democratic or otherwise. This is now beginning to change. Far from quiet acceptance of unpopular laws, peoples in many countries now demonstrate and demand change. With the exception of those countries under tight military rule, the people, more and more, are demanding to be heard, to have their needs addressed, and bad laws righted. As the beneficent energies of Aquarius gain in potency, this growing power of the people will multiply and become the most powerful voice on Earth. So much is this the case, even now, that governments of all kinds are forced to take account of the peoples' reaction to laws which deeply concern their welfare. It becomes increasingly difficult for governments to govern along strictly factional lines. Much government action is secretive and obscure, much is done 'behind the scenes' of which the people never hear, but generally, governments, at least in the so-called 'democratic' world, are careful not to rouse the ire or discontent of the people.

There is one major area in which this is assuredly not the case. For over sixty years, governments worldwide have withheld from the people the reality of 'UFOs' or 'flying saucers'. Further, they have sought by all means to denigrate the occupants of these visiting craft as 'aliens', destructive and harmful to the people of Earth. To keep their populations under

5

control, and to avoid 'panic', they have denied the experience of hundreds of thousands of intelligent, open-minded citizens. They have thus created a major myth: "'Flying saucers' do not exist but they are dangerous and rapacious to men of Earth"! Likewise, they have taught the people to deride the notion that crop circles are a legacy from Space, yet every government has unassailable proof of the existence, creativity and superior technology of these brave and harmless visitors from the sister planets of our System. Our profound ignorance of the subtle planes of matter has allowed the major governments of the world to maintain this deception for so long.

At last the time of revelation has arrived. For no longer will government agencies hide the truth from men of Earth: their brotherhood with the far-off planets of our Solar System. Already, the "star-like luminary", the Herald of Maitreya's emergence, is showing people worldwide that for years they have been deceived by their governments. You may be sure that Maitreya will reveal the truth of our relationship with the other planets, and of the co-operation which for long has continued between us. It is in truth the time of revelation.

(Share International, July/August 2009)

UFOs and Their Spiritual Mission

The following article is an edited version of a talk given by Benjamin Creme at the Transmission Meditation Conference held near San Francisco, USA, in August 2009. Published in Share International, January/February 2010.

There is an enormous amount of information of one kind or another about UFOs, some of it true, absolutely authentic, and masses of it utterly unreal and unauthentic. This is a huge and all-important subject.

I am going to refer to an article by my Master , "The Time of Revelation", which sets out the position very clearly.

In the late 1940s and early 1950s pilots of all types of aircraft, sometimes with their passengers, began to report that they had seen inverted saucer-like objects with domes and circular windows, which flew alongside their plane and then sometimes sped off at tremendous speed. These reports gained in currency and became headlines in various newspapers. When I first read about them, I assumed like many that these saucer-like objects were probably new craft that had been made by America, Russia or Germany. After the end of World War II, the Allied armies moved into Germany. In southern Germany obvious, demonstrable evidence was found that the Germans had been carrying out secret experimentation in anti-gravity devices during the war. At the same time, the Americans and Russians were carrying out similar experiments in secret. All of them were fiercely engaged in an anti-gravity approach to flight, which was entirely new.

However the true nature of these extraordinarily advanced saucer-like craft was about to be revealed. In 1953 an Englishman, Desmond Leslie, wrote a book, *Flying Saucers Have Landed.* He was a gifted man (a cousin of Winston Churchill) who wrote plays, novels and music. Before the book was published he heard about a man living in the USA, George

Adamski, who had written an article in which he claimed that he was in touch with people from other planets. Adamski said that a group of observers could vouch for his meeting with a man from Venus.

One day, by arrangement, in November 1952, Adamski went into the desert, near Desert Center, California. The group of observers stayed a few hundred yards away and viewed the scene through binoculars. A spacecraft landed, of the type that flew alongside the planes in the 1940s and 1950s. According to Adamski a man came out of the spacecraft dressed in a one-piece suit. He communicated to Adamski without using language; in fact, they had a telepathic rapport. The man, who said he came from Venus, was wearing shoes the soles of which were cut in such a way as to leave clear and pronounced impressions in the desert sand, which were later photographed by the group who were watching from a distance.

The word was put out that a man from Venus had landed in a spacecraft. Leslie heard about this incident and wrote to Adamski, suggesting that Adamski add his sighting report in the desert to the book that he, Leslie, had already written about the history of flying saucers down the ages. Leslie's book claimed that flying saucers from other planets had been visiting Earth for thousands of years, and that there were many descriptions of these craft, and artefacts on Earth, that lent weight to this claim. Leslie and Adamski together published the book *Flying Saucers Have Landed* (1953) and it became a best-seller. Thousands of copies were sold all over the world. The information was taken up in a big way by the so-called 'New Age' movement, especially in America. Adamski went on a series of lecture tours in the US, South America, Europe and elsewhere, talking about the spacecraft.

In 1955, Adamski published another much longer book, *Inside the Space Ships*. In that book he gave an account of having been taken up in a small scout craft, like an inverted saucer with a dome, to a huge mothership. Inside the mothership he was introduced to extraordinary people, and given profound teachings by a major figure on the ship, a teacher from Venus.

That teaching was so profound it changed the thinking of thousands of people who read the book. It was not the only source of that teaching, but was very much akin to that given out by the great teachers of this world, such as Krishna, the Buddha, the Christ, and Mohammed. All the great religious teachings seem to be underscored by and validated by that given by the teacher from Venus. It is profoundly transforming and closely resembles Maitreya's teachings today, for example when He talks about the oneness of humanity, the need for sharing, justice, right relationship, and above all, the utter necessity for peace. This is emphasized over and over again in the teachings given by both Maitreya and the Venusian teacher. Adamski, a straightforward, genial individual, brought this teaching back home and made it known.

It fits together perfectly with the core of New Age teaching, given by our spiritual Hierarchy through Helena Petrovna Blavatsky, Helena Roerich and Alice A. Bailey. This gave a new different understanding and hope to humanity as it emerged from the horrors of the Second World War. The effects of the war were still being felt very strongly in Europe, Japan and Russia, and people were just beginning to pick up the threads of civilization again. They were looking for meaning and purpose, for guidance in the restructuring of the world.

The United Nations was formed, and in it was embedded the creed of the rights of men and women everywhere, the United Nations Declaration of Human Rights. The world gradually faced up to the problems that had accrued as the result of the war – for example the poverty of Germany, which was absolutely shattered by the Allies, and the extraordinary damage and loss of life that had occurred in Russia, which set back the Russian people from their desire to create a new society after the terrible struggle with Nazism.

After the war, America created the Marshall Plan, its greatest act in many decades. This transformed European industry, supplying Europe, especially West Germany, with the newest and best applications of industry that America, despite the war, had been able to create throughout the war years.

Space Brothers assist during crisis

Then came two traumatic events. Berlin was divided into four zones: the Russian, American, British and French. In 1961 the Russians blocked their zone, making free passage between eastern and western Berlin impossible. America and Russia had been allies in the war against Nazism from 1939 to 1945, but became enemies in the most extraordinary ways. America held on to its idea, if not complete, of democracy, and Russia to its idea, if not the reality, of communism. Each held fanatically to these two ideas and brought the world to a point closer than it had ever been to a Third World War. These two major powers had just emerged from the second part of the Great War of the 20th century and in 1961 stood at loggerheads.

What few people know is that President Kennedy did not bring about the cessation of hostility between Russia and America at that time. It was brought about by the Space Brothers of our own solar system, chiefly from Mars and Venus. They are masters of energy, as can be seen in the exploration of space by the UFOs. They have a control of energy such as we do not even know is possible, and were able to nullify the tension between the Americans and Russians.

President Kennedy was advised by a Venusian agent living on Earth to approach the Russians in a certain way, which he did up to a point. He did it – in his own American way, but he did it – and in the meantime the Space Brothers completely removed the energy from the situation and the crisis passed. That was the nearest point since the war to a breakout of a third world war and was only prevented by the Space Brothers. They called on all their forces, their own control of energy, and all those who live among us as ordinary people but who are actually agents of Venus, Mars, Jupiter and other planets.

In October 1962 there was another point at which the world came close to a third world war. In September, the Soviet government had secretly delivered nuclear missiles to Cuba. When United States intelligence discovered the weapons, the US government did all it could to ensure the removal of the missiles. Then, in October, the Russians chose to call America's bluff. They sent a ship loaded with more nuclear missiles across the Atlantic en route to Cuba, on America's doorstep. The Russians made no attempt to camouflage them this time, so anyone could see they were missiles. It was an answer to America, a provocative attempt by Russia to say: "You have surrounded Russia with missiles from Alaska to Pakistan," which America had done and still does. Pakistan is an American base, and has been for years. From there, as well as from the southern border of Russia, up to Alaska, Russia is completely surrounded by the missile bases of America, and has been since the 1960s.

President Kennedy for a second time made an announcement. He had been told by the Space Brothers, through an agent in the US Diplomatic Service, what to say. He did more or less say what he had been asked to say but again in his own way, rather than in the way he was asked to say it.

As he had been asked at the time of the Berlin crisis, President Kennedy was again asked to speak to the Russians with respect and understanding, saying that he could clearly see their concerns and would seek to allay their fears. Instead, he was very outspoken and challenged Russia. I do not believe the Russians had any intention of continuing to deliver these missiles to Cuba. I do not believe they were so foolish, so lacking in insight, to think that they could do this without being stopped. Certainly the Cubans had no wish to be obliterated from the face of the Earth. So the ship turned back, as Russia, I am sure, had expected it to do in any case.

That was the second time the Space Brothers had to intervene very strongly to bring about a cessation of animosity. They do this by energy, by nullifying the negative forces, allaying the fears of the people, and bringing about the possibility of a truce, a state in which new things can grow. That is how the Space Brothers have worked all along.

They do not believe in confrontation. The advice given to the people of Earth is to solve all disputes by co-operation rather than confrontation, seeing the other point of view and taking the spiritual path rather than the path of war. That is the nature of the Space Brothers. They are so evolved that they never have wars. They are way above that and have nothing but peace and goodwill for humanity.

Humanity lives not only in this solar system, but also throughout the whole of cosmos. There is nowhere you can go in cosmos where you will not find human beings.

The solar system and the Plan

All the planets are engaged in one Plan, which also involves Earth. Most people on Earth do not even know that such a Plan exists. It is a Plan of evolution for our solar system, which works as a unit.

We think of the Earth, the Sun and Moon, but pay very little attention to the other planets of our solar system, except through NASA and the Russian exploits. All the planets have their Plans. They are all part of our solar system and the solar system evolves together.

Not all the planets are at the same point in evolution. Some are very low in evolution. Some, like Earth, are about halfway along the path. Some are very evolved indeed. As we have hundreds of thousands of lives to go from being an early animal man or woman to a Master, so a planet has seven expressions or rounds, each of which is millions of years long. Some planets have completed that course and have become invisible, but are still there, in etheric energy. Some, like Venus, are in their last round. Venus is the alter ego, the higher aspect, of Earth. Earth is about at the halfway point, in the middle of the fourth round. At that point a planet begins to find its course, its destiny. Its people begin to wake up. This is happening in the world today. Humanity is waking up from a long sleep in which it lost contact with reality, with the purpose and meaning of life on Earth. It became deeply embedded in the profound materialism in which it is still involved to this day.

Maitreya has come to awaken humanity. The space people too have come to help and save humanity. They have been portrayed, most particularly by the US government, as bestial beings who destroy carcasses and leave them strewn over the plains and deserts of America, who take people up in their spaceships, perform operations on them, embed little chips that keep the people under their control ever afterwards, and send them back down to Earth. All of this is utterly false.

If one thing is clear from the teachings of Adamski coming from the Venusian Master, from my Master, and, you will find, from Maitreya, it is that the Space Brothers are absolutely harmless to the people of Earth. In fact, their presence here is a spiritual mission. They come to save humanity from even greater pain and suffering than we would otherwise have known in the years since the discovery of nuclear fission.

Since that time we have poured nuclear energy into our atmosphere, which our scientists cannot even measure. They do not have the technology to measure levels of matter above gas, the etheric levels, where this release of nuclear energy occurs – the deadliest release of energy that has ever taken place on Earth.

This nuclear energy is in tremendous potency and is destroying the well-being of humanity and the lower kingdoms. It works by depleting our body's immune system, and therefore opens us to all manner of ills that otherwise would not affect us. As a result, we have wave upon wave of influenzas and other diseases that we have less and less ability to cope with. The growing incidence of Alzheimer's disease at ever younger ages throughout the world is a direct result of the high concentration of nuclear energy at the higher etheric levels, not registered by the instruments of our present-day scientists. This energy plays on the human brain, causing more and more Alzheimer's, memory loss, disorientation, and the gradual breakdown of our body's defence system.

The Space Brothers, mainly from Mars and Venus, are engaged on a spiritual mission to neutralize this nuclear radiation. They are not allowed to completely neutralize all the extant nuclear radiation, but within the karmic law they do, using various implosive devices. They neutralize the radiation that we are pumping into the atmosphere from every nuclear power station without exception, and from all nuclear experimentation. We are continually making more and craftier bombs that will be more deadly than previous bombs. All of that experimentation releases into our atmosphere clouds of nuclear radiation that we do not know about. We cannot measure it and therefore we deny its existence.

Our nuclear scientists believe they have total control of nuclear energy, which, demonstrably, they do not. They have no understanding of the four etheric levels of matter above the solid, liquid and gaseous levels and therefore a limited knowledge of what they know as nuclear energy. It is actually etheric, physical matter which we should not be using. Nuclear energy is, as it says in the Bible, "that which stands where it ought not". Nuclear fission should not be utilized. It is deadly and is increasingly damaging the health of the people of this planet. The people of other planets spend countless hours mopping up this energy.

At the same time they are creating on the dense-physical plane a replica of our planet's magnetic field. Every planet is surrounded by a magnetic field. It is made up of lines of force that criss-cross, and where they criss-cross they form vortices.

These vortices have been replicated on the dense-physical plane by our Space Brothers as part of a new energy grid that Maitreya calls the Science of Light. This energy grid in relation to electrical energy brought directly from the sun will give us the new Science of Light as predicted by Maitreya. It will give this planet, as on other planets, unlimited, safe power for all purposes, in ways that cannot be bought up or cornered by any group of men.

For obvious reasons, this technology will not be given until we have abandoned war for ever. Most essential today is that we should abandon war for ever, come to a co-operative agreement among all people that war is a thing of the past. This will be the basic point of Maitreya's early teaching. He will stress again and again that we have to make peace. Nothing short of peace will do because we can now destroy all life, human and subhuman, on planet Earth. Maitreya and the Masters come in part to make sure that we do not destroy our planet.

If we did destroy the planet, it would have irrevocable consequences for the rest of the solar system, and the future for humanity would be dreadful indeed. We would have no planet to live on, and would have perpetrated a terrible crime against ourselves and the other planets. We would end up incarnating on some distant, dark planet, not at all evolved. We would have to start at the beginning, as we were millions of years ago, and take again the long slow climb upwards. It would be unbelievably painful and restrict our evolution for thousands, perhaps millions of years. Why choose that? Why, indeed, choose such an end?

The nature of the Space Brothers is to serve. They make great sacrifices to help our planet. In their thousands they have come, and they spend their time and energy helping us in every way.

They create vortices which are visible as crop circles to be sure, but also invisibly across the world in general. The crop circles are only an outer tangential sign of their presence. If you have the eyes to see, this sign tells you that someone of tremendous intelligence, skill, tact and reserve has touched the edges of our garment, and said: "We are here."

They could land, make a big noise and tell us that they are here, but they do not. They make contact quietly, sensitively – so that they do not drive us to panic. If they come down and people panic and are terrified, the Space Brothers just go away. If the people are not terrified, if they do not panic, then things might happen. The Space Brothers might introduce themselves, and they have introduced themselves, to thousands of people of this Earth. These are people who to this day have never mentioned their meeting with a spaceship and with spacemen who came out of it, who spoke to them without seeming to speak, but made them understand that they were visitors from far off planets come in peace to help us. The people who have been contacted have been afraid to speak, afraid to be ridiculed.

We ridicule those who speak out. We ridicule those who tell the truth, even when we recognize it as such. We tend to reject the truth because it means a change in oneself, in one's way of thinking, feeling, acting and reacting. It means a real psychological change, so it is difficult. It is easier, therefore, to deny than to affirm.

Even when people could affirm, because they more or less believe what they read about the Space Brothers or about the Reappearance of the Christ and the Masters, they tend to reject it. They tend to find reasons to deny or belittle it, or to demand proof that will only come through time. They want proof that will only come when the Space Brothers come down, open the doors of their ships, walk out and say: "Hi." Then they would believe because everyone would see them and it would be easy to believe. But when the Space Brothers make contact in the quiet, calm and gentle way that they do, contacting one here, two there, those who are contacted do not have the courage to say: "I saw with my own eyes and therefore cannot deny it."

Governmental ambivalence

Sometime in the mid-1950s I went with some friends to the Air Ministry in London and asked them what their take was on flying saucers. We were ushered into a long office. Behind the desk were shelves absolutely covered with books, all of which had "Classified" boldly printed on the cover. We met a pleasant young man; he was a spokesman for the Air Ministry, and therefore could talk to the public.

We asked him: "What is the official line on flying saucers?" He said: "Well, we have a lot of books. All these have classified information in them. I cannot show you the books, but take it from me they have reports from pilots, policemen, and so on, thousands of reports about flying saucers, but only reports. They are not proof; they are reports. Our take on flying saucers is that they do not constitute a threat to the security of this country [the UK]."

"So they do exist but they are harmless. They do not constitute a threat."

"Oh, no. We do not say they exist. We say they do not constitute a threat to the security of this country."

"That would be difficult to do or not do if they did not exist."

"We are not saying that they do not exist, but we are not saying they do exist. We are only saying they do not constitute a threat to the security of this country."

The telephone rang, and he said a few words into the phone. Then he said: "Excuse me, I have to go. I shall only be away for 10 minutes or so." He went out, and of course we were on the books immediately, reading all about the classified information! He was out for about 15 minutes. I think he had himself called out, so that we would have a look at the books. He told us what was in them so we indulged. We heard him coming back and closed the books.

"Well, I am sorry," he said when he returned. "That is all the time I have. I have work to do."

We went away quite happy that they had not said the extraterrestrials are evil, dangerous monsters who want to eat people!

Maitreya's 'star'

It has now become clear that southern England is the home of crop circles. More crop circles are appearing year after year in southern England, mainly in Wiltshire, but also the surrounding counties. This is where the best crop circle photographs come from.

An Englishman, Steve Alexander, hires a helicopter and takes photographs of the crop circles as soon as they appear. This year [2009], about two or three weeks ahead of the usual time for crop maturity, the first crop circle that was made was in the form of a 'star'. It was in the form of a star – a circle and radiating lines coming from it in all directions – because of Maitreya's 'star'. This is a further sign that the Space Brothers are indeed involved in what is happening in the world.

Maitreya's 'star' is not a star, of course. It is what my Master called "a star-like luminary of brilliant power". It is one of four spaceships, two from Mars, one from Venus and one from Jupiter. They are in each of the four corners of the Earth – north, south, east and west – and become visible in the daytime and night-time. They are seen for a time and then they have to go to recharge their batteries, which they do directly from the sun. Then they come back into position again. They pulsate and move up and down and sideways, twist and turn, behaving very unlike any planet or star. They have a brilliant light and change colours all the time, from blue to red to green to yellow to violet to white, over and over again. In this way they are acting as the herald of Maitreya's emergence into the open, His first television interview in the USA, which will be very soon. (See Page 83.)

The Space Brothers are totally involved in Maitreya's emergence. These four craft have been specially called upon. They are huge, each about the size of five football fields put together. Because of that they seem large compared to a twinkling star. They look nearer the size of a large planet like Venus or Jupiter. Sometimes people have seen Venus or Jupiter and thought it might be the 'star'. Other times they have seen the 'star' and have been told by those who are supposed to know better, like astronomers or those consulted by media when asked, that it is probably Venus, Arcturus, Sirius or any other bright star or planet. These 'stars' made by Space Brothers will remain there until the Day of Declaration.

Maitreya is emerging very soon. The Day of Declaration could be anytime from a year to two or three years after His first television interview. The Masters and Maitreya Himself seem to think that the time will be relatively very short indeed. But whatever the timing, these four spacecraft will remain in the heavens, seen by an increasing number of people. Hopefully the media of the world will become more and more open to reporting on these 'stars'.

Already a slight start has been made in the media. As well as numerous videos on YouTube, there have been reports in Norway and Mexico. There was a recent report in Japan on nationwide television lasting one minute 47 seconds, which is quite a long time in television. It showed a craft jumping up and down, going round and round. The reporter is saying: "Well, what can it be? What can it be?" The man who took the video is interviewed and seems perfectly honest, so the whole thing is an "interesting mystery". We want more of that kind of "interesting mystery" in the media until it is taken seriously.

[Note: In December 2009 much media attention was given to

the Norwegian spiral light confirmed to be one of the four 'stars'.]

Meanwhile there has been a tremendous coming together of the Forces of Light of this planet, the Hierarchy of Masters and initiates, and our planetary brothers in the rest of the solar system, who are coming to this planet in their thousands. Where one UFO was perhaps seen some years ago, 10 or 12 will be seen; where 20 were seen, hundreds will be seen; where hundreds were occasionally seen, thousands will be seen. In the last year there have been reports of tremendous armadas of spacecraft going slowly across the sky in South America, the Far East and Europe.

Very recently, almost a stone's throw from where I live, some 15 spacecraft were seen at night going across north London. People stopped, got out of their cars, and looked up. There was a big fuss about it in the newspapers for one edition and then nothing after that.

The number of sightings will continue to increase. More and more people will come into contact with the Space Brothers, have experiences and be encouraged to speak out. It will become clear that all over the world men and women in their thousands have had experiences of the flying saucers and for the most part have been too shy, too afraid of ridicule to speak.

I have been engaged for the last 35 years in preparing the way for the reappearance of Maitreya as head of the Spiritual Hierarchy of this planet. A similar kind of Hierarchy exists on every planet. On Venus, which is so evolved, there are Masters Who are like gods. Indeed, They are gods.

My first work with the Spiritual Hierarchy was not for the reappearance of the Christ and the Masters of Wisdom per se but with and for the Space Brothers. I was not, as I saw it, preparing the way for the return of Hierarchy to the world except insofar as the work of the Space Brothers is part of this. They too are preparing the way for the manifestation of Maitreya. They are working with Maitreya daily, hourly, moment to moment.

Today we have evidence of the Space Brothers all around us. The crop circles have been growing in complexity and beauty for years. The British Ministry of Defence, who said that they do not look on the flying saucers as presenting a threat to the security of Britain, nevertheless to this day bribe farmers in the south of England to destroy the crops, as soon as a crop circle appears in the field.

I talked to a farmer once as we were standing in a crop circle. He said: "They tried to bribe me and I would not do it. They will never get me to accept their money. I think it's terrible. I do not know what this means, to be honest, but I know it means something very, very important. No harm has ever come to me and my family in having these crop circles on my land, and I will always continue to resist this bribery."

Other farmers have taken the money and probably still do, so some crop circles are lost. But it shows that the Ministry of Defence are not really honest about their attitude to the Space Brothers. They have kept the information out of the public eye as far as they are able.

I was once talking with some friends about the Space Brothers, and someone said: "I do not disbelieve it. I would believe it if I could see a flying saucer."

"Would you?"

"Yes, if I could see one, I would believe it."

I would sometimes ask flying saucers, if they were nearby, to show themselves. I would say: "If there is one in the vicinity could you make an appearance?" And sometimes they did. So, on this occasion one immediately appeared. They watched it go across the street, over the buildings opposite and they said: "A spaceship." It looked like a light moving quite slowly, very gently.

The first one I ever saw was on one evening when I was sitting indoors and suddenly had the feeling that I was in touch with the pilot of a spaceship that was coming up above the River

Thames. I could feel him coming up the river. I had no reason to think this but I thought: "He is coming up the river, and if I go out maybe I can see it." I went out to the corner of the road and saw a spaceship coming very slowly, with a shining light moving slightly up and down as if it were floating. It was fuzzy and had an oval shape. It went slowly up and over beyond the houses in total silence. I felt I was in touch with the mind of the pilot. But it was not the pilot. My Master gave me the thought that the spacecraft was coming up the river.

I remember being in north Wales once with my wife and a friend. We were out walking in a big open space not far from our hotel and our friend said: "Oh, I wish I could see a flying saucer."

I said: "Would you believe it if you saw it?"

She said: "Yes, I would believe it. If I could see it with my own eyes, of course I would believe it."

I said: "Well, hold on." I asked, if there is one in the vicinity would they please show themselves? Within a second, a fantastic sighting took place. It came from my right, and looked just like the sun only smaller. It was shining like the sun, glowing bright, golden yellow. It tore across the sky above us at terrific speed. It was at about 2,000 feet and continued on until it was over the trees and the horizon. We have a saying: "Their mouth fell open!" I had never seen that before, but our friend's mouth did, literally, fall open.

I said: "There is your flying saucer."

She said: "Is that what it was?"

"Yes."

"It was not a plane. I have never seen anything like it before."

"No. It was a spacecraft. That is what they are like."

"Are there people in it?"

"Yes, there are people in it."

"Can you contact them just like that?"

"Yes, I can sometimes." We walked back to the hotel. She

ran ahead and rushed into the bar, where the hotel owners were. She shouted: "I have seen a flying saucer! I have seen a flying saucer! Well, at least Ben said it was a saucer. But it couldn't have been. It just could not have been a saucer. No, it could not have been. No."

She had just had the most wonderful sighting and did not believe it. I had never had a sighting like that. It was only about five or 10 minutes later that she said: "It could not have been."

"Well, what was it like?"

"It was like the sun."

"Was it a plane?"

"No, it was not a plane."

"Was it a balloon?"

"No, not with that speed."

"Sounds like a saucer."

"No, it could not have been a saucer."

Today we have crop circles, the preparations for the Science of Light, and we have the 'star', the herald of Maitreya. We also have patterns of light which appear on buildings throughout the world. There seems to be a new phase now in which the people in the UFOs respond to human thought and request. If you see UFOs and ask them to move, to prove that they are spacecraft, for example, as often as not they do. They answer the call, the appeal. Try it for yourself.

They are looking for people who are not afraid. For some reason many people are afraid. They believe the stories put out in the press about the 'monsters' in flying saucers, ready to ravage and tear them to pieces, put things in their arm and perform operations on them. It is sad because it has made us afraid of these harmless people.

The space people are harmless in a way that we only wish human beings would be. We invade each other's privacy all the time. We have no reticence. They are reticent, quiet, polite, in a way that most of us are not.

Living together in peace is Maitreya's call. That is how the Space Brothers live – harmlessly, tactfully, respectfully. They are our Elder Brothers, as are Maitreya and the Hierarchy of Masters. We are one solar system. All of us are engaged in a journey to perfection together. We are at different levels, some nearer the end of the road, some of us struggling to find a path to the right road even after millions of years.

The Space Brothers are here to help. With their help the forces of evil will be destroyed, the forces that prevent people everywhere from living together in peace with justice and right relationship. Right relationship is the next destined step forward for humanity, and with the help of the Space Brothers and the emergence of our own Hierarchy of Masters, that will quickly come to be.

The Space Brothers are giving of Their knowledge of the Science of Light, the new Science that will give us unlimited energy for every need. They have that science, and will put it at our disposal, as soon as we renounce war forever, showing that we are able to live together in peace with justice, sharing, and right relationship. Then we will know that They are our brothers indeed.

THE GATHERING OF THE FORCES OF LIGHT

by the Master —, through Benjamin Creme

Important events are taking place in many parts of the world. People everywhere will be astonished by the reports. These will include sightings, in unprecedented numbers, of spacecraft from our neighbouring planets, Mars and Venus in particular. Nothing like this increased activity, over vast areas of the Earth, will have been seen before. Those who have steadfastly refused to take seriously the reality of this phenomenon will find it difficult to deny. More and more accounts of contact with the occupants of the spacecraft will add their testimony to the fact of their

24

existence. Miraculous happenings of all kinds will continue and multiply in number and variety. The minds of men will be baffled and amazed by these wonders, and this will cause them to ponder deeply.

Into this wonder-filled, wondering world Maitreya will quietly enter and begin His open work. He will be asked to counter their doubts and fears, to explain these happenings and He will vouchsafe their validity. These extraordinary events will continue unabated and cause many to prophesy the ending of the world. Maitreya, however, will continue in His simple way and interpret differently these events.

Thus will Maitreya encourage men to see the marvellous breadth and scope of life, the many layers of which man knows but little till now. Gently He will introduce them bit by bit to the basic truths of our existence, the Laws which govern it, and the benefits achieved by living within these Laws. He will acquaint man with the vastness of our Galaxy and show that, in time, men of Earth will conquer Space and Time. He will encourage men to seek within, as well as without, for the answers to their problems, and validate their constant connection to each other and to Cosmos. He will remind humanity of its long history and of the many perils which man has overcome. He will sow the seeds of faith in our own illustrious future and vouchsafe the eternal divinity of man. He will show that the path of life, the evolutionary journey, leads unfailingly upwards as well as for ever onwards, and that to make the journey together, as brothers and sisters, is the surest way and the way most lit by joy. Look, then, for the signs of Maitreya's entrance, make it known, and uplift the hope of your brothers.

(*Share International*, March 2007)

Who are the 'Forces of Light'? (November 2009)
We think of the Forces of Light as the Esoteric Hierarchy: the Christ and His group of Masters, Who make up, with all of Their

disciples, the Forces of Light of our planet. There are 63 Masters connected with the human evolution, including three Great Lords, one of Whom is Maitreya. They are gathering together a host of people from all over the world to work with Them in this coming time. Some are already working with Them, others will come. There is a huge new group formed by Maitreya in 1922, called the New Group of World Servers. There is no outer address where you can join. You are picked according to your attitude to life. There are 4 to 5 million people already in this group; it consists of a small inner group who receive instruction directly from the Masters and a much wider group who receive instruction indirectly and gradually from their own soul. They work in every field, in every country: in politics, economics, science, religion, the arts, education and so on. They are responsive to humanity's needs.

In the early 1930s in one of the Agni Yoga books (published by the Agni Yoga Society) Maitreya Himself said: "There was a time when 10 true men could save the world. Then came a time when 10,000 was not enough. I shall call on 1 billion." Some years ago I asked my Master: "Has Maitreya got His billion people yet?" He said 1.5 billion, so already He has half a billion more than He needed then. The number is now 1.8 billion. These people are also part of the Forces of Light. He will call on all those whom He knows beforehand will respond to Him and will teach others to respond. It does not take the whole of humanity to respond to Maitreya but a certain proportion, a critical mass.

What is the purpose of this frenzy of UFO activities particularly in the UK but worldwide in recent times? (November 2009)
It is all part of the "gathering of the Forces of Light". Our planetary Forces of Light are added to by spacecraft from our neighbouring planets, which you rightly said are coming in ever greater numbers. We are part of a solar system, an integrated unit. My Master wrote an article in March 2007 in which He

talked about the coming together of the Forces of Light: both from this planet and from our sister planets in the system. That is why we are seeing so much UFO activity. The spacecraft are real and come from Mars and Venus, mostly, but also from Jupiter and Saturn and other planets.

Most people believe what they are told, that there is no life on Venus or the other planets, but the spaceships, the UFOs, have been seen by thousands of people for years, mainly from Mars and Venus, which are the nearest planets to us. The governments of the world for over 60 years have denied the existence of UFOs, which indeed in growing numbers are active in our skies. The governments have hoodwinked the public for their own reasons, probably mixed. They have sought to deny the existence of UFOs, flying saucers, whereas people who have seen them know that they are always present in our skies.

What is the motive for this curious non-exposure of a tremendous event? The governments would say they want to avoid panic, but beneath that is the unacknowledged fear of loss of control and power, which a welcoming approach to the Space Brothers would ensure. They know that if humanity knew that the spacecraft in our skies were not 'aliens' but were here to aid and alleviate the suffering of humanity on this planet, and with their obviously far more advanced technology, people would demand that they are openly welcomed and their superior teaching made available to them.

Earth scientists deny the existence of any form of life on Mars and Venus and the other planets of the system. This is the result of their inadequate understanding of the true range of matter. These scientists acknowledge three planes – solid, liquid and gaseous physical – above which, they have not the technology to measure. Therefore they believe 'more' does not exist, yet the Masters and all students of esotericism know that there are four further states of matter above gas, the etheric planes of matter. It is on the etheric planes that can be found 'life' on all our sister planets, from Mars, on the lowest etheric level, up to extraordinarily advanced planets like Vulcan, Venus, Jupiter, Saturn, and so on. Venus, the alter ego of Earth, is in the last of its seven 'rounds' (equivalent to our incarnational experiences), while Vulcan is completely perfected.

Spacecraft from these planets create the crop circles of which the largest number are seen in Wiltshire, the southwest of England, because Maitreya is in London. These crop circles are the 'calling cards' of the people who man the UFOs, to acknowledge that they are here, without alarming people or infringing our free will. The craft are designed so that they can make in seconds the most complex design, covering several hundred yards in diameter, so advanced is their technology.

Maitreya, when asked, will talk about the Space Brothers. They are our brothers and sisters of our own planetary system. The Hierarchy of all the planets work together in an interplanetary parliament.

THE SPACE BROTHERS' WORK ON EARTH

In what ways do the inhabitants of our sister planets help humanity? (July/August 2009)
The first thing to understand is that UFOs, Unidentified Flying Objects, may be unidentified by the government agencies, but they are real, they exist and they have a mission. Without their help this planet would by now be uninhabitable. There are people on all the planets of our system. The Masters of our planet are in touch with the Masters of the various planets and the solar system acts as a unit. The planets are not isolated but are in contact moment to moment, and they evolve together. If one falls behind, as this planet has done, it causes concern for the others.

The beings in the UFOs, from whatever planet – mainly Mars and Venus but others too – have a tremendous task in working to eliminate, or at least reduce, pollution. Pollution is the greatest threat to humanity. More deaths are caused by it than by any other cause. It brings about the breakdown of our immune systems and therefore opens us to all sorts of illnesses to which we would otherwise be immune.

The space people are concerned with making this planet habitable. They go through our skies mopping up and neutralizing large amounts of the nuclear waste and the general toxic filth that we pour into the atmosphere. They are not allowed by karma to clean up the planet completely, but within karmic limits they do so. Otherwise life on this planet would be very painful indeed: more people would be dying than are dying, more people would be suffering from Alzheimer's, and daily we would be more and more asphyxiated. So we owe the Space Brothers a tremendous debt.

Another part of their tremendous work for planet Earth is that they are replicating, on the physical plane, the magnetic energy field around the planet. The energy field is made of flows of magnetic energy and where these flows meet and criss-cross a vortex or centre of force results. They are replicating that centre of energy in connection with a new technology which will give us unlimited, safe energy for all our needs direct from the sun: the 'science of light', which is the technology of the future. It is obvious, therefore, that far from being 'alien', malicious monsters to be feared, as they have often been presented to the public, the Space Brothers are on a spiritual mission to help in every way possible within the Laws of Karma to maintain the stability and future health of planet Earth.

What is the nature of the Space Brothers' spiritual mission? Will they be teachers, for instance? (March 2010)
They are teachers in a sense. Through Adamski they have given quite a body of teaching, especially from the Venusian Master on the mothership in Adamski's book, *Inside the Spaceships*. This

Master's teaching is close to that of Maitreya. It is about the relationship of man to man, and man to what we call God, the spiritual nature of all beings throughout cosmos. That is teaching, but they do not come out onto the platform and put out leaflets or write books, not that kind of teaching.

The Space Brothers do not come to penetrate every aspect of our lives. However, they will do what we cannot do and will show us how to do it, for instance in the fields of the new technology and the science of light. They will not work directly as our teachers; they have their own evolution and we have ours.

Somewhere in the Bible it says something about Chariots of the Gods. Would this be a reference to UFOs as we know them? (June 2009)
Yes, precisely.

Apart from those from Adamski, are there any other teachings that come from the Space Brothers? (March 2010)
This is like every aspect of New Age thinking. It is a minefield and you have to pick your way very carefully through it all. There is authentic teaching such as that of Adamski but there is also a tremendous amount of glamour and illusion.

What is the purpose of the Space Brothers' underground bases on this planet? What are they doing there? (March 2010)
We have despoiled everything on this planet. All land, air, rivers, sea and oceans are polluted. The spaceships go down into the depths of the ocean and neutralize the pollution as far they are allowed. We have stored nuclear energy waste in the Atlantic and Pacific, and the Space Brothers do their best to nullify the effects of these terrible sources of toxic waste, so they have a lot to do. It is an ongoing process. They work in a similar way underground, which we have also saturated with our chemicals and nuclear waste. They have devices which can neutralize the

worst elements of pollution, particularly that of high-level nuclear radiation. But they are limited by the law of karma in how much they are allowed to help us.

Are the Space Brothers involved in healing work? Will they have any role in Transmission Meditation or are they somehow connected with Transmission Meditation? (March 2010)

Do they have a healing role? No, not per se. Are they involved in Transmission Meditation? No, not directly but they are transmitters of cosmic and planetary energies to our Hierarchy, Who distribute them through Transmission Meditation groups. They do not interfere in our life. They come to help. It is a rescue mission in which they are involved to save planet Earth, and to save humanity from the terrible havoc that we have caused through nuclear radiation and all the ravages of the Earth, the forests and so on. It is a planetary mission rather than interfering in our daily lives.

Will the Space Brothers help to teach us about the art of living? (March 2010)

Indirectly, yes. They have a lot to say about the art of living, particularly the God-like emissaries from Venus. The beings of Venus are extraordinarily evolved. Sanat Kumara, the Lord of the World here on Earth, comes from Venus. The space people have much to teach humanity, but then so have our own Spiritual Hierarchy, Maitreya and the Masters. I do not think it is a question of choosing between this or that body of teaching. You will find it is all very similar. It is just difficult to do – or seems difficult to us.

Will the Space Brothers eventually have a public role in relation to humanity like the Masters do? (March 2010)

The answer to that has to be no, but it is a qualified no. They do not want to take the place of our own Hierarchy. Anything they do in the future in relation to helping Earth will be done from behind the scenes, showing what can be done. If necessary, they will be active agents of the new technology that they are helping to make real on Earth. This will happen when the time is right, when we have accepted certain principles, in particular the total abolition of war.

They have a role, but they will not take the place of our Hierarchy. They are too polite, too aware of the occult axioms, and too aware of how to live in relation to other people, to infringe our free will by taking over. They will have an advisory status only on Planet Earth. They have come to help; that is it.

Why are the Space Brothers helping us here instead of focusing on their own planet? (March 2010)
They are conscious members of the alliance that is the confederation of planets of our own system. They work not just for their planet or for any other planet, but for the growth and perfectionment of the system as a whole. That system is the body of expression of the Solar Logos. If their work entails helping Earth, so be it. That is what they do. If it were another planet, they would do the same.

What is our relationship to Mars that brings them here to help us? (March 2010)
It is a neighbouring planet at about the same level of evolution as Earth, although technologically far more advanced, so they can be of help. They like to help fellow planets who are lagging behind, who are in trouble, who are misusing nuclear energy and causing the planet and themselves to suffer. They have a great heart and wish to help humanity. They do it out of love.

According to a Second World War veteran, who was in the Royal Air Force, he had many UFO sightings during the war. There was this phenomenon of so-called "balls of light", foo-fighters, accompanying the aircrafts which were going to bombard

Germany. Pilots thought those lights were secret weapons of the Germans. But German pilots saw the very same lights when they came to England, and they thought it was the secret weapon of the British. Could you explain what these lights were? (July/August 2004)

All the space vehicles have listening devices, which may be two or two-and-a-half feet in diameter, and they can be directed from the spaceship itself, which might be about 30 feet in diameter. These devices are sent down and connected energetically with the mothership, and they have instruments that can read the reports, which are fed into very advanced computers. Our computers are ancient, backward things compared with the technology they have; these pick up data on everything: the quality of the air, the thoughts and ideas of individuals, if necessary. They may hover outside a room here and listen to this conversation, for example. Following an aircraft, they cannot be shot down – they have a force field round them. The spaceships, too, cannot be shot down – they also have a force field round them. They have often been fired at by fighter planes sent up to intercept them but there is no way the rounds can penetrate the force field of the ship, so it is a waste of time and energy.

These foo-fighters do a job – I cannot tell you what the job is in every single case, it will vary from time to time. They use different devices for different purposes, but very common are the small disks for carrying information. I have seen them; I have ducked as they come so close! They do not mean any harm; it is just a kind of "hello".

The India Daily newspaper reported many people from areas affected by the Asian tsunami seeing UFOs a few days before the catastrophic event. People in the Indian state of Tamil Nadu, India's Andaman and Nicobar islands, and Indonesia's island of Sumatra reported seeing strange flying objects in the sky. In Port Blair, the capital city of Andaman Island, tourists saw silent flying objects. Remote areas of Bangladesh, Myanmar and Sri

Lanka also recently reported UFO sightings. Were these genuine sightings? (January/February 2005)

These sightings were authentic reports of UFO activity. The spaceships were from Mars and were assessing the growing earthquake tension/pressure and the possibility of a tsunami.

Scientists on the Setihome project, which searches for signs of life in outer space, believe that a signal from space picked up three times by the Arecibo radio telescope in Puerto Rico may be a "message from another world". Is the signal (named SHGbo2+14a, and located between the constellations Pisces and Aries) a deliberate communication, a signal emitted by an astronomical object, or radio interference or a system fault? (January/February 2005)

It is a deliberate communication from "another world".

In 1908 a massive explosion took place over Tunguska, Siberia. It registered over 5.0 on the Richter scale, was equivalent to 15 megatons of TNT (1,000 times the atomic bomb that devastated Hiroshima) and levelled 1,000 miles of forest. Research later showed that the explosion took place five miles above the Earth's surface. There were similarities between the Tunguska explosion and a nuclear blast. At least 169 hypotheses have been suggested as to what caused the explosion. However, the most prevalent is that a meteor, comet or stony asteroid exploded. (1) What caused the explosion? (2) Did Maitreya or the Space Brothers intervene to guide the object over the sparsely populated Siberian forest in order to spare the lives of countless people elsewhere? (March 2007)

(1) It was a huge meteor. (2) Yes. The Space Brothers intervened.

CONTACTING THE SPACE BROTHERS

Was President Kennedy aware that the person advising him during the crisis points in his presidency was from Venus? Was

Adamski involved? (March 2010)

President Kennedy was not aware of the Space Brothers per se, nor was he aware of the source of information. But he was aware of certain individuals in the diplomatic corps of America who were agents of the Space Brothers. He thought highly of their advice and information, and acted on it. It was always given through that agency in the diplomatic service. Adamski himself was not actively involved.

Likewise, President George W. Bush, when he was in office, was informed by such an agent in the diplomatic service that there would be an attack on America – the White House, the Pentagon and major buildings – which came to pass on 9/11. They were warned three months in advance of this event and did nothing about it. That is the extraordinary thing, the difference between President Kennedy and Bush. Bush was told not to react to the events of 9/11. Of course, the first thing he did was to react immediately in the wrong way and he declared an impossible war against 'terrorism' which has soured international relations ever since. He discoloured his eight years of office by invading Afghanistan and Iraq, and he turned America from a reasonably open democratic society to a near fascist state.

Do the leaders in the world know about the Space Brothers openly and quite explicitly? (March 2010)

There are leaders around the world who believe in this phenomenon, and do not know why the leading countries like America, Russia and the European nations fail to make it known. They do not want to do it themselves because they do not want to be out of step. But they think it is perfectly believable that the UFOs are from some place, not necessarily Mars or Venus, but some place outside our solar system. None of the UFOs in fact come from outside our solar system. They come from the planets of our own system. These leaders may not know that, but they do believe in the existence of UFOs and in some cases would like to make it known. The South American countries, especially Brazil, have suggested that the truth should be told, but nothing has come of it.

Are there any Space Brothers working in the United Nations or in any governments? (March 2010)
In the United Nations, certainly, yes. In any governments? Yes, in some but not as many as you might think. Not in positions of power, but usually in advisory positions, in the diplomatic corps of various countries, for example.

Are we going to make closer contacts with UFOs? (July/August 2004)
Yes. The Hierarchies of all the planets are in communication. This is something which people should understand. We ourselves do not have that communication but Hierarchy does. Hierarchy is made up of Masters of different levels and of disciples of even more varied levels. And from all these disciples, all these different grades of initiates, some may be part of groups who have been working with the Space Brothers. The Space Brothers have on this planet various people, like Adamski and others, who are used to bring the reality of the Space Brothers to the world, but also for other reasons, which I cannot go into; there are various aspects of this work which must be kept secret, for the time being at least. They have a great work in salvaging, in helping to restore the equilibrium of our planet.

You mentioned that there are different individuals who work together with UFOs on different projects. There is an interesting project in America, conducted by Dr Steven Greer called the 'Disclosure Project'. Could you comment on this? (July/August 2004)
Dr Greer is doing useful work. He is not working – so far as I know – with the Space Brothers but he is impatient with the fact

that there is enormous evidence to prove that UFOs exist – not proof of where they come from, or their purpose, but that they are real, do, in fact, exist. They have been seen by hundreds of thousands of people for years, and yet the governments of the world, most of whom have adequate data on their existence, refuse to make that known.

There is a huge cover-up, from the highest levels, in America, Russia, Britain, the European and various other countries who have been collecting data, evidence from their pilots, policemen, soldiers, and the public for years. This amounts to a huge body of evidence which is never published, never made known but is covered up. People disappear even, in certain parts of the world, and nothing more is heard of them. There is even sometimes coverage by media to discredit the evidence, and so on. In this way the governments control what the public knows, or rather does not know, about the Space Brothers and the UFO phenomenon. In this way they can keep it down.

Dr Greer is impatient with this, he has himself experience of UFOs and wanted to make it known. He has set up a means for other people – ex-army, ex-RAF or ex-United States Air Force personnel – to come forward and give their evidence. When people of their standing and experience give evidence in this public way, they hope it will lead to a general, better understanding and maybe eventually an open statement by the governments of the world.

Of course, when governments make such a statement about their knowledge, they are also at the same time committing political suicide. They think that if we know the technology that the Space Brothers have, which is so much more advanced than our own, then the ideas, the wisdom of these people is much more to be valued than that of our own governments. They do nothing but make war on each other, in competition destroy the economies of each other, and make life miserable for hundreds of millions of people throughout the world. Inevitably, we would say we want the Space Brothers to come and teach us their ways, that we do not need you, Mr So-and-So and Mr So-and-So. They see that as a loss of their power, and so they keep the whole thing dark.

How can we contact the Space Brothers? (March 2010)
Can we contact them? No. They contact us. They know those on whom they can depend, who can do the work that they are engaged in and that needs to be done, who can commit themselves and work like they do.

Is there any way in which we can contribute to their work? (March 2010)
You can contribute to their work by making them known, by giving a true picture of them and their work. If you can present them as people who do exist, in spaceships that do exist, and that they are totally harmless and peaceful beings who only come to help, you would do a good job for humanity.

Can the space people in the UFOs we see increasingly in our skies 'hear' us? Can they telepathically hear that we would like to see them as we stand scanning the night sky? Can we ask them to show themselves to us? I would really like to meet some of our space brothers and sisters! (September 2008)
Yes, but as often they record reactions of fear in those who observe them.

Have the Space Brothers gone through the human evolution in their process? Have they taken group initiation? (March 2010)
Some have and some have not. It depends on who you are talking about. They are not just one type called a Space Brother. Each planet is at a different point of evolution – some very different, others minimally different. There are space people who have, in common, gone through various levels of initiation and

others in which it does not arise. They are perfected. Initiation as we have it on our planet is really an artificial means of speeding up of evolution. It is not found everywhere.

How many Space Brothers live among us at this time? How do they manifest? Are they born into a family as a baby or come as an adult? (March 2010)

My information is that they number around 2,000. They are all over the world in very many countries. Some visit this planet on a temporary basis and come for a few hours, a few days or a week or two. Others take up long-term residence and come in different ways. They might come as a fully-grown adult. They might take incarnation through a family and grow up as a child.

Adamski was a grown man before he realized that he was not ordinary. There is an interesting book by Desmond Leslie called *The Amazing Mr Lutterworth**. It is out of print, but I think it is possible to get hold of second-hand copies.

The book is a fictional account based on the life of Adamski. Lutterworth is a Venusian, but he is in an Earth body.

Desmond Leslie, who knew Adamski very well, revealed that Adamski had, instead of a navel, a half-inch deep star, actually a circle with brilliant lights radiating from it like a star – Venus. This, of course, you could not tell until he raised his shirt, but he did show it to Leslie.

Adamski was born in Poland, and came to America as a child. His parents were Polish immigrants. He grew up in the USA, lived a long time on Mount Palomar in California, and eventually died in the US.

The book makes very interesting reading. It tells the story of someone who has a growing awareness of what most people are not aware of – other people's thoughts, for instance. He is invaded by all the thoughts of those around him. Sitting on a bus, he can tell what the people around him were feeling and thinking, and he is appalled by it. It is terrifying, but gradually he gets it all under control. The book is fiction but based on what Adamski told Desmond Leslie of his own personal experience. [*Note: A book review, an article, and questions and answers regarding Adamski were published in *Share International* October 2008.]

What is the reason for these people from other planets to incarnate on this planet? (March 2010)
Because they can do their work more cogently and intelligently over a period of time by taking a physical Earth body than they could just by temporarily lowering the vibration of their own body. For that period of time they become part of Earth.

One way this happens is to 'fall', as it is called, make a spiritual fall from a higher to a lower state. They might fall from Venus or Mars or some other planet to Earth and incarnate on Earth as an ordinary person.

Many people have done this, usually very advanced people like Leonardo da Vinci, Shakespeare, Bach and Beethoven. Maria Callas was a modern example. Various people at that sort of level have incarnated on Earth and they then go through the evolutionary process.

You have explained that William Shakespeare and Leonardo da Vinci were Avatars from Jupiter and Mercury respectively, and that they had been with Earth humanity for many centuries previous to their famous incarnations. So they must have had a much more humble point in evolution when they started their journey on Earth. (1) Was it foreseen at a much earlier stage in their evolution that in the future they would be able to fulfil some important role on Earth? (2) Or did they fall to Earth, and then after doing very well here, get chosen to play the role of Avatar? (3) How many Avatars are there on Earth right now? (4) When you say they 'fell' to Earth, does this mean that their karma compelled them to be put on a less advanced planet? (November 2008)

(1) No. (2) People are not chosen to 'play the role' of Avatar. They are either Avatars or not. If they fall to Earth they have become 'Earthly'. (3) Twenty-four. (4) Yes.

How would you recognize a Space Brother if you saw or met one? (March 2010)
You would not necessarily recognize him at all unless he wanted to make himself known to you or he wanted you to recognize him. If he were an undisclosed worker for the Space Brothers, he would just appear as an ordinary man to you. You could not tell him apart as being or not being from another planet.

Do the Space Brothers appear in a kind of mayavirupa? Do they create it themselves? (March 2010)
No. They take a body on this planet and are born as an ordinary person. That is, if it is long-term. If it is very short-term, they lower the vibrational rate of their body until they are vibrating more or less at the same level as we are. They seem to be just ordinary beings. But that is temporary. If it is long term, they will incarnate into the world and work 'sotto voce' – quietly – in that way. That was how Adamski worked, for example.

(1) Would it be useful to have some sort of group invocation that might elicit a sighting of the Space Brothers? Is there an alignment or place to hold our focus when trying to contact the Space Brothers? (2) What is the best way to invite the Space Brothers to appear? Using Maitreya's hand? Using mental focus on the ajna centre or other centre? Would a flight upon a craft or ground visit or ship tour be honoured if requested? (March 2010)
(1) The glamours rise up! A mantram that will invoke the Space Brothers? What will you do with them when you invoke them? Wave? (2) Every word of this is glamour. Forget it. Your job is not to go cruising on flying saucers. Your job is to make known that Maitreya, the Christ, the World Teacher, is emerging with

the Hierarchy of Masters. That is the task you have set for yourself. It is not to get the thrill of a spaceship ride or to waste the time of the space people in giving you their attention. How would you go up in a spaceship? You are solid physical, and they are not. How would you do it?

After reading your information regarding so-called UFOs being from Mars and Venus, I wonder how this can be possible. The surface temperature of Venus is over 800 degrees Fahrenheit. Mars has been photographed by satellite for a number of years and recent probes have found no sign of life. However, I can see how this would be possible if the UFOs were from a higher dimension than the physical, emotional, and higher mental planes and were able to step down from that higher dimension (plane) into the physical (world). Is that what has happened? (September 2007)

Yes, this is almost precisely what happens. The physical plane, as understood by our scientists, has three levels only: solid, liquid and gaseous physical. In fact, it has seven levels, the top four being etheric, and to our sight invisible. To Martians, Venusians and other Space Brothers, they are not only visible but are their normal, physical level of being. The UFO vehicles are also made of etheric energy and would normally be invisible; but they do lower the vibration of the atoms of the vehicles to bring them in range of our sight. This is a temporary manifestation only.

If Space Brothers live on the etheric plane how do they manifest on the physical plane so that we can see them? (March 2010)

It is a temporary thing. When a Space Person comes to Earth and wants to be seen he has to lower the vibration of his etheric body to come within our range of sight. The same applies to the spacecraft. These vehicles are made of etheric physical matter and if you do not have etheric vision they are invisible. But they are seen by hundreds of thousands of people all over the world when the occupants lower the rate of vibration of the vehicle.

(1) Can life in the higher etheric matter be detected by sound through conventional instruments? (2) Is the ability to hear the sounds of energies considered 'etheric hearing'? (3) Do other kingdoms in nature, such as animals and plants, exist in the higher etheric matter on other planets, such as Mars? (March 2004)

(1) Yes. (2) No. (3) Yes.

What has happened to the British space probe Beagle 2, which was supposed to land on Mars on Christmas Day 2003? Did it crash, or is it lying in a crater where its transmissions have not been picked up? (March 2004)

It crashed.

Regarding the two spacecraft recently sent to Mars by NASA: (1) Are Earth's scientists who are involved with the Mars project receiving any help from 'higher' scientists such as those on Mars? (2) Will they make any surprising or significant discoveries? (3) Was there ever a dense-physical life on Mars? If so, how long ago? (March 2004)

(1) No. (2) Yes. (3) Three million years ago.

PLANETARY EVOLUTION

How can it be that people on another planet on the etheric planes with higher technology than we have could be less or only as evolved as we are? (March 2010)

It depends on the planet. Mars, for example, is at about the same stage as Earth. Every planet has seven rounds lasting very many years. Some planets, like Earth, for example, and Mars, are in the middle of the fourth round. Some planets are perfected. Some are almost perfected. Venus is in its last round.

43

On Mars there are three levels: A, B and C. On A, the top stratum, the people are like gods, perfect beings. In the middle stratum there are well-evolved people but not yet perfected. On the lowest stratum, C, the people are not very evolved.

Mars has not made as many mistakes as we have, which is why it has a technology unbelievably ahead of ours. They are masters of space, masters of energy. They make most of the spacecraft we see and call UFOs, from small scout ships up to gigantic motherships. Even some of the Venusian spacecraft are made on Mars to Venusian specifications. They are in etheric matter and are all made by thought. We might think that Mars is a very evolved planet because of its advanced technology, but in terms of planetary evolution it is in the middle of the fourth round, as is Earth.

Would the people in the C stratum of Mars travel to other planets? (March 2010)
No. They are not allowed to travel.

I have a question about the Earth being in the fourth round and Venus in the last round. I never understood what that meant. In the human, physical field I cannot imagine what this means. (March 2010)
Our soul incarnates hundreds of thousands of times. In this way we evolve from early animal man and woman up to a Master and finish the school that we call Earth. You may not think of it like that, but the experience of Earth is the experience of relinquishing the need to incarnate, the spiritualizing of the nature of the planet. This is a dense-physical planet and we are in dense-physical bodies, so it is more difficult for us to imagine the true nature of humanity. We are not dense-physical bodies except from one point of view. We are really light. But that light takes form on this planet as our dense-physical body, astral body and mental body.

As we evolve through the five initiations, we draw more and more energy from the soul into the body in each incarnation. This means we are drawing subatomic matter, which is light, into the body, and the body gradually changes. The first initiation starts the enlightening of the body. The second degree initiate draws some light into the body. The third degree initiate draws more. The third initiation is called the transfiguration, and the body becomes a purer vehicle for the soul. The fourth degree initiate draws even more light, and the fifth initiation is possible when the body is completely transfigured and transformed. That is resurrection, and all the Masters are resurrected beings.

The person is really divine for the first time after they have taken the third initiation, and is dedicated to the work of service to the world. They become creative in a way that is not possible before – however creative they might be as a second- or even as a first-degree initiate.

The planetary path of evolution is something similar: instead of incarnations, the planet has rounds. A round is a cycle. Instead of thousands of incarnations that the soul has in the human evolution, the planets have seven major cycles, millions of years long. Over that period of time, in our sense of time, the planets

There are planets that are in the first, second or third round. Earth is in its last round, the seventh. I do not know how long it will be until it is complete, maybe many thousands of years yet. Both Mars and Earth are in the middle of the fourth round, at which time the planet 'awakens'. Enough has gone on before for the awakening of the true spiritual nature of the planet to become evident to the people, and more and more people are perfected. In that amazingly pregnant point in the middle of the fourth round everything starts afresh. A culmination is reached in the growth aspect and there comes the outpouring of the genius of the particular planet, its qualities, its gifts, and the development of the people in a new way. We are in that stage and

20

* * *

so is Mars. Mars is more advanced than Earth because they have not made as many mistakes. We have made mistakes all along. We have fought wars since the beginning of time on planet Earth.

People wonder why Maitreya does not come forward, but they do not know how Maitreya's work is held back. They do not know how the planet is threatened from negative forces in our own and other lower planets. These stimulate the negativity of the Earth. They use people who can be used, and wherever possible they make mayhem, making it difficult for this planet to proceed on its evolution and for Maitreya to come forward into the dense-physical world of everyday. It is a fight. There are people on this planet, some very well known and very powerful, who are agencies of these dark forces.

For example, the majority of the wealth of this planet is owned by relatively few people – families, corporations, institutions. Naturally they make every effort to hold on to the power that this gives them. So it has been throughout the ages on this Earth. It holds back the evolution of the planet. This is what we know as the forces of materiality.

(1) You have said that only on planet Earth can human beings exist with gross physical bodies. Is this the reason planet Earth was chosen to express the physical body of the great Third Ray Life (p99 of Esoteric Psychology, Volume Two)? (2) Does the above make us particularly vulnerable to the influence of the Lords of Materiality? (3) Does the Earth humanity have a special role in spiritualizing matter? (May 1995)

(1) Yes. (2) No. (3) No. The inhabitants of all planets have the role of spiritualizing matter (at its various levels). Earth humanity does this at the dense-physical level also.

(1) How exactly did humanity 'lose its way' 98,000 years ago, and (2) how will humanity now 'find its way' again? (May 2001)

(1) This refers to the end of the Atlantean civilizations, which had lasted for 12.5 million years. Gradually, having been following a steady spiritual path for most of that time under the stimulus of the openly-present Spiritual Hierarchy, humanity became polarized into those who continued on the spiritual path and those who became more and more enthralled by the Lords of Materiality (commonly called the forces of evil). A great war ensued. The Masters of the Hierarchy decided to retire to the mountains and deserts where Their groups still, for the most part, live. From that time, humanity has slowly sunk deeper into materialism (in the broadest sense). We are now faced with the major crisis of our history: a crisis essentially spiritual but focused today through our political and economic systems. (2) Under the teaching and stimulus of Maitreya, humanity will come to understand how deeply materialistic and unspiritual are our institutions, values and ways of living. He will inspire us to see that sharing, justice and freedom for all are prerequisites of spiritual life.

Are there any spaceships from outside our solar system that visit Earth? (March 2010)

My information is that there are not. Because it has been posited that life is impossible on the other planets of our system, some people, even with fairly authentic contact with the Space Brothers, insist that they come from outside our solar system – usually from the Pleiades. I personally do not believe this to be so. There is no overt contact between our civilization and that of the Pleiades.

Negative Propaganda against UFOs

If we speak to people about the 'star' and the spaceships, they often say that people are abducted and are left with scars and implanted chips. How do we refute this? What can we say to make it clear to others about what you are saying? (March 2010) It is just not true. It simply does not happen. There are many people who go to science fiction films and see presentations about extra-terrestrials as evil, scheming monsters seeking ways and means of taking over Earth. If this were the intention of the Space Brothers, they could have taken over every city of the world long ago. These disturbed people have vivid astral imaginations which are as ephemeral as dreams, which they relate to their frightening experience of those science fiction films. These astral imaginings become widely accepted due to the general denigration of the Space Brothers and their vehicles by governments and other agencies for over 60 years. There is an agency in the United States that has as its sole purpose the distortion of the reality of the UFOs. The United States government, like all other governments, knows that UFOs exist. They know from experience that they are harmless. They probably know that they have important work to do. The governments of the world would love to have all the technological secrets from the Space Brothers, and at the same time they want to keep from their people the evidence that proves the Space Brothers to be harmless, beneficent, helpful and so superior to the governments under which people live here on Earth.

If the Space Brothers are so advanced, and their technology tends to show that they must be, then we, the public, would say: "Who wants the government of America, Britain, France, Germany or any other known government in the world? Let the Space People come, land and tell us the secrets of their success. Then we can maybe go the same way."

The governments know that this is what people would do. They would lose the power over the people that they have at the present time. They are also afraid of panic, because they have sown so many seeds of hatred, violence and mysterious occult practices in the minds of the public about the Space Brothers.

Orson Welles made a radio adaptation of HG Wells' book *War of the Worlds* in 1938. When he announced on that programme that planet Earth was being invaded from Mars, for days people were absolutely terrified. They believed that they were being invaded from space, that the Martians were already zooming down and about to drop their lethal bombs. The programme was only a joke, a very irresponsible joke, but that was Orson Welles. Governments have sown the seeds and carry on with the process of increasing the fear that they have already sown in the minds of people of Earth, in their own countries and abroad.

There are so-called abductions. Should one take them seriously? What is the truth of this in relation to UFOs? (July/August 2004) No one is ever abducted in a spaceship. Those who say they are abducted have experiences of an astral-emotional nature in which they imagine that they are in spaceships. Nobody is ever taken up in a spaceship in a physical body. It is impossible. These spaceships are not solid physical. To be taken up into a spaceship you have to be taken out of the dense-physical body and you go in the etheric into the spaceship, which are in themselves etheric. It is still physical, but etheric physical.

Now, people say they are taken up and experimented on, things are put into their skin and so on. The Space Brothers know all about us, they do not need to do this. To me it is a nonsense, because they are so advanced in every way that they do not need to make any kind of experiment. They know the answers already. It is a complete nonsense that they should carry out genetic or sexual experimentation on people from this planet when they have a technology which is several thousand years ahead of anything that we could think of today. It is stupid, a deliberate way of attacking the concept of wise and superior, spiritually oriented people. In this way, the people in control in, or even behind, the governments of the world retain their power.

Who is doing the cattle mutilations? (March 2010)

As I have said, there are agencies, particularly in the USA, whose job for many years has been to denigrate the Space Brothers. They are government agencies but not necessarily known to the officials of the administration. I would doubt that recent presidents of the USA know anything about this agency and its work against flying saucers. They would find it hard to believe. Those people mutilate cattle, scatter them around the pastures and the deserts, and then blame it on those 'aliens' from space. They are up to every nasty trick to keep this dark. Some of them do it, I think, for fun. They vie with each other in thinking up things to do to denigrate the Space Brothers.

They are experts in their particular line of work, which is to do with corrupting human minds into disbelieving something that is so obvious and true to hundreds of thousands of intelligent people. They will go on with this until they see that they cannot do anything more. They are now coming to the end of their ability to keep this reality a secret.

How much does the desire for power and control figure into the reason that the governments have been keeping UFO information from the public? (March 2010)

It is paramount. It is ignorance and fear that drives the governments to act as they do. They understand that if humanity knew that the Space Brothers really existed, and these spacecraft with such a command of space and time really existed, we could ask them to help, because our governments obviously do not know what to do. They could advise and teach humanity. Who needs governments like we have today when we have these beneficent, harmless beings waiting to help us?

Will governments come forward and acknowledge the Space Brothers? (July/August 2004)

The governments will only act when they are forced to do it.

When Maitreya is known openly, He will be asked questions like I am being asked now, and the truth of the relationship between this planet and the other planets will become known. Then the people from other planets will land and the reality of their existence will be known.

In the first place, the knowledge, the acceptance of the reality of the Space Brothers, will come through the acceptance of Maitreya and the Masters of our Spiritual Hierarchy. They will confirm that the Space Brothers are real, that the spaceships are real, that the other planets have their citizens who have nothing but goodwill, who are harmless, who want to help each other, and who help this planet in so far as the law of karma allows. When we accept them and see what they are doing and how they are helping us, the development of this planet will proceed apace.

The Vatican seems to be saying publicly that life might exist on other planets. Is the Vatican easing its flock into the notion that life exists on other planets, that UFOs and all accompanying phenomena are real? What's behind this policy? (July/August 2008)

Quite simply, yes! The truth is beginning to come out and the Vatican cannot afford to seem unaware of the obvious.

What would be the impact on humanity's consciousness of knowing about the existence of life on other planets and the fact that the Space Brothers are here to help us? (March 2010)

It would have an enormous impact. For educated people in the hundreds of thousands who believe in flying saucers, who have seen them and charted their movements, who have come to southern England, stood in the crop circles and felt the energies in the different circles (the energies of Martian and Venusian crop circles are different), for them it would just be a vindication of what they believe already.

But for the mass of people who do not know what they believe, it would be a revelation. They might at first be frightened of the idea because of the way it has been presented, but they would soon get over that when nothing negative happened.

How can we overcome the tendency of the major media to marginalize the story about the Space Brothers? (March 2010) Obviously you cannot. Time and events will do it of themselves. You just have to put out the information about Maitreya and the externalization of the Spiritual Hierarchy, and the part that the Space Brothers play in this extraordinary event.

Now that the Space Brothers are present, in what ways can we consciously interact with them? (March 2010) Now that they are present? They have always been present. How are they now present in a way that they were not before? I have spoken and written about them for years and so have many others. I have emphasized the return of Maitreya and the Masters to the world. That is the paramount information which I have been asked to make known.

Before that I worked with the Space Brothers. When asked, I have always included all or some of what I know of the Space Brothers. I have never sought to hide the fact of their presence or belittle their role in this work.

The coming of Maitreya and the reality of the Space Brothers are linked together. It is not one or the other. Our work has always been to emphasize the fact of Hierarchy's return to the everyday world. But they do not return alone. They return with the help in many ways of the Space Brothers. Both our Hierarchy and the Space Brothers have a spiritual aim that is at the basis of all their actions, whether they are from this Earth, Mars, Venus or the other planets.

Why is it important now to release the information on the Space Brothers? Why is this the "Time of Revelation"? (March 2010)

It is the time of revelation because until now their existence has been relatively unknown and denied by governments and the media. The activities of the Space Brothers are increasing all the time. The latest manifestation is the 'star', the herald of Maitreya's appearance in public. When presenting the 'star' it is impossible to avoid presenting it as a spacecraft and when Maitreya is asked on his public interviews about UFOs, He will openly acknowledge their reality.

GEORGE ADAMSKI AND OTHER CONTACTEES

*Desmond Leslie co-authored the book **Flying Saucers Have Landed** (1953) with George Adamski. In the book Leslie tells of an experience he had while on his way to the British Museum. He had the sudden urge to enter a bookstore that sold rare and unusual books. A gentleman in the store came up to Leslie and said that he would be interested in a certain book that the gentleman happened to have in his hand. The book was about aerial craft that were used during Atlantean days and was just what Leslie was currently interested in for his book. The man was described as having penetrating eyes that seemed to look into one's innermost being. May I ask if this man was a Master, a Space Brother, both, or someone else entirely?* (July/August 2005)

The man was Maitreya.

*I recently read a wonderfully informative and inspiring book by George Adamski called **Inside the Space Ships**. His description of the love, wisdom and superior intelligence of the Space Brothers is chastening; their ability to live in harmony with Universal Principles, with a sense of the Divine in all beings and in all objective life is thrilling. My question however: is some of his information (perhaps only in some details) imagined?* (May 2002)

No, it is all Adamski's direct experience inside one of the Motherships. The only thing he omitted to say was that he was out of the body during the whole experience. In a person of Adamski's level, he would consciously leave the body and in full consciousness enter the new situation. He would return to the physical with full memory of what he had experienced. These spaceships and their crews are essentially of etheric-physical rather than dense-physical matter. The crews can lower the vibrational rate to come within our vision threshold but only on a temporary basis. The particular Mothership in George Adamski's account was Venusian, manned by Masters from Venus, but was actually made on Mars.

*Before he rose to world fame with his books **Flying Saucers Have Landed** (1953) and **Inside the Space Ships** (1955), George Adamski wrote a novel entitled **Pioneers of Space: A Trip to the Moon, Mars and Venus** (1949). Sceptics have claimed that he took "fictional material" from this book and presented it as fact in his later books, as his own experiences. (1) Could it be that Mr Adamski described actual experiences in his first book that he didn't remember as such because they took place outside his waking consciousness? (2) Or did he present his own experiences in a novel first to test the public's reaction to the idea of life on other planets?* (April 2007)

(1) No. (2) Yes.

*Giorgio Dibitonto claims in his book **Angels in Starships** (1990) that he was taken on board a spaceship by his extraterrestrial contact, Raphael, who introduced him to Orthon and Firkon (alien contacts of George Adamski's) and a Space Brother named*

George Adamski
Photo: © AFU

George who, according to Raphael "lived for a while on Earth, where he chose to come on an assignment". (1) Were Mr Dibitonto's experiences real or imagined? (2) Was the Space Brother he met the same as the one we know as George Adamski? (3) Did he indeed meet Mr Adamski's alien contacts known as Orthon and Firkon? (October 2008)

(1) Real, but out of the body. (2) The same being. (3) Yes.

*In his book **The Pawn of his Creator** (1995), Henry Dohan writes that George Adamski was prepared, under the guidance of an initiate, for his future mission as a witness of the existence of extraterrestrial civilizations. As Adamski's father had died when he was still a child he was taken under the wings of a friend of the family whom Adamski referred to as "Uncle Sid" and who arranged for him to go to Tibet as a teenager to study with the Masters. (1) Was "Uncle Sid" a Space Brother or an initiate? (2) Did Adamski indeed go to Tibet for several years to study with the Masters?* (October 2008)

(1) Both. (2) Yes.

*The poetic quality, the rhythm and the colour, of 'The Prelude' in George Adamski's last book, **Cosmic Philosophy** (1961), seem to me reminiscent of the writing of a Master. (1) Did this Prelude, entitled 'The Magnificent Perception', and/or other parts of this book, indeed originate from a higher source? (2) Was it perhaps inspired by the Venusian Master Whose teachings Adamski recorded in his book **Inside the Space Ships**?* (October 2008)

(1) Yes. (2) Yes.

George Adamski describes the form of motherships (spacecrafts) as cigar-shaped. Are the 'stars' similar? What kind of craft are they? (December 2009)

Many of the larger spacecraft which work to our benefit are cigar-shaped but some are bell-shaped, some are fish-shaped and some are saucer-shaped. The 'star' heralding Maitreya's presence is also a spacecraft able to transform into different shapes and colours.

Q. (1) What are the point in evolution and the ray structure of George Adamski (1891-1965), who lived in California, USA, and who had contacts with space people around 1950? (2) Are there still space people living among us, as there were then? (March 2004)

A. (1) Soul: 2; Personality: 4 (6); Mental: 1 (4); Astral: 6 (2); Physical: 7 (3). He was 2.0 degrees initiate. (2) Yes.

*From the information which the Space Brothers give in Mr Dibitonto's book **Angels in Starships** (1990), it would seem that most, if not all, of the angels and many of the prophets in the Old Testament were Space Brothers. Could you comment, please?* (October 2009)

None of the prophets were Space Brothers but were members of the Earth's Spiritual Hierarchy. Some of the 'angels' were indeed visitors from other planets.

The 'cosmic blessing' which Mr Dibitonto describes in chapter 15 of his book involves Space Brothers whom the author refers to as "the Blessed Lady" and "the Lord", in a thinly-veiled reference to the Madonna, and Jesus or the Christ, respectively. Was the event which Dibitonto described here attended by the Master Who was the Madonna and the Master Jesus? Or were They Space Brothers of much the same 'standing', if one can use that word here? (October 2009)

They were the Master Who was the Madonna and the Master Jesus.

On several occasions the Space Brothers are said to warn of catastrophic events which await mankind because of its wrong thoughts and actions, reminiscent of the biblical Apocalypse. Could it be that the Space Brothers rather warned about the collapse of our present outmoded structures, while the author interpreted these warnings according to his own (apparently Christian) understanding of events surrounding the Second Coming? (October 2009)

No. They were warning against the catastrophes of global warming and the degradation of our environment, the planet.

ENCOUNTERS WITH SPACESHIPS

A very well known UFO encounter took place on 5 November 1975. Seven lumberjacks were driving home from working in the Apache-Sitgreaves National Forest in the state of Arizona, USA, when they spotted a "golden disk" about 15 or 20 feet in diameter hovering silently 20 feet off the ground. One lumberjack, Travis Walton, approached the craft. While he was about six feet under the craft a blue-green ray was beamed at him from below the surface of the craft. As he lay unconscious his fellow lumberjacks sped off fearing for their lives. For five days Walton was gone, during which time there was an extensive but fruitless search. When Walton returned he claimed that he had been abducted by "aliens". Your information is that no one is abducted by the Space Brothers and that such claims are the result of an overheated astral imagination. However, seven people witnessed the event. (1) What is the real story? (2) Are there shadow aspects to the military and government in the US who actually kidnap people and put abduction experiences into their heads to cause fear about the Space People and so keep the truth hidden? (March 2006)

(1) This was a genuine encounter with a Martian spacecraft. Walton was not abducted but was invited and came aboard of his own free will. He was taken out of the body, which was rendered invisible and protected, and taken on to a mother ship. He had a wonderful (in both senses) time. He was later brought back to his body. He was asked to make known his 'adventure' but I am afraid he did not feel able to do so. He was afraid he

would be ridiculed or worse. (2) Yes. The military are behind the abduction stories for the most part.

In 329 BC Alexander the Great noticed several shining, shield-like objects emerge from a river in India. He was convinced he witnessed otherworldly vessels. (1) Were these real UFOs? (2) Alexander the Great spent the remaining six years of his life searching for these craft in a diving bell. Some speculate that he was trying to find and conquer the only kingdom that eluded him thus far: Atlantis. Did Alexander the Great indeed have grandiose illusions about conquering Atlantis? (March 2006)

(1) Yes, from Mars. (2) No, but he wanted to find the source of these 'otherworldly vessels'.

On the morning of 7 February 1989 around Los Angeles, California, several people, including divers and those standing on shore, witnessed a large, dark object emerge from the ocean and release about a dozen smaller craft. The object descended back into the ocean and was tracked on radar (or sonar) travelling south toward the Santa Catalina Channel. (1) Was this UFO a large 'aircraft carrier' type of spacecraft? (2) What planet did this craft originate from, if it was a real UFO? (3) Do the Space Brothers have bases in the world's oceans or under the oceans in the Earth and possibly even between Catalina Island and California? (4) A phenomenon known as 'USO' (unidentified submerged object) refers to UFOs in the oceans. Do the Space Brothers travel the seas as effortlessly as they do the atmosphere? (March 2006)

(1) Yes. (2) Mars. (3) Yes, many. (4) Yes.

There is a theory called 'worm hole' that suggests there are places within the universe where space and time fold together in some fashion and where it is possible to travel the vast distances of space in a matter of seconds. We have heard that time and space is an illusion, so is this theory accurate at all? (June 2007)

It is not that space and time 'fold together' but actually more simply that time and space at a higher level do not exist; they are an illusion. Those Who are already masters of Space – the Space Brothers – can travel enormous 'distances', as we think of it, in seconds of 'time'.

On 10 June 2004 in Guadalajara, Mexico, a fleet of around 100 UFOs were videotaped. Were these real spacecraft and, if so, what planet did they originate from?

On 5 March 2004 a Mexican Air Force airplane with the 501 air squadron was doing a routine patrol of Mexico's southern border. They picked up an aircraft on their radar and began to pursue it. The crew turned on their FLIR (forward looking infra-red) system to help locate the craft. Soon the FLIR system caught numerous glowing objects, at times up to 11, navigating around the airplane. This incident garnered much media attention in Mexico. Were these genuine spacecraft and, if so, what planet did they come from? (March 2007)

In both cases the UFOs were spacecraft from Mars.

On 24 April 1964 a police officer, Lonnie Zamorra, in Socorro, New Mexico, USA, heard a loud roar like an explosion. He drove to a nearby area where there was a dynamite shack, thinking it had just exploded. Instead he witnessed an oval-shaped object. The object had landing gears as well as a ladder extended to the ground with two small child-sized people outside. Upon seeing officer Zamorra, they entered the craft and it immediately departed. (1) Was this vehicle and the two people outside the craft from one of the planets in our solar system and, if so, which one? (2) You have said that the craft used by the Space Brothers are indestructible. However, were they having 'engine trouble' so-to-speak or (3) did they land and manifest themselves in dense-physical form so officer Zamorra could see them and pass along what he saw to others? (March 2007)

(1) Yes, from Mars. (2) No. (3) Yes. The explosive noise was simulated by the occupants of the craft to attract attention.

There seems, from all internet and general media reports, to be a lot of UFO activity over Latin American countries. Why is there so much UFO activity there? (April 2007)

Actually it is not confined to Latin America. There is an increase in UFO activity in many parts of the world. This will continue on an increasing scale up to and beyond the emergence of Maitreya into the open.

On 17 April 1981 a Japanese freighter, the Taki Kyoto Maru, was sailing off the coast of Japan in an area of the ocean known as 'The Dragon's Triangle', when the crew felt something equivalent to shockwaves course through the ship. A bright, saucer-shaped USO (Underwater Submerged Object, or a UFO under the water) about 50 feet in diameter arose from the ocean. The ship's dials, compass and engine 'blurred'. The USO circled the ship for about 15 minutes and plunged into the sea causing massive waves that nearly capsized the Japanese freighter. The time on the radio in comparison to the time on the crew's watches showed that the crew lost 15 minutes.

(1) Why did the equipment 'blur' when the UFO came near? (2) Why did the crew experience a loss of 15 minutes of time? (3) Is there anything in that area such as an underwater UFO base that could cause electromagnetic disturbance and distortions in time, or was it perhaps old Lemurian technology still operating under the sea etc? (November 2007)

(1) This is usual in such encounters. The effect of electromagnetic 'swamping'. (2) The same reason. (3) Yes, a UFO base (not Lemurian technology).

(1) Is anyone receiving messages from "the Brotherhood on Sirius"? (2) If so are they publishing them? (3) If we come

across printed material containing what is claimed to be Sirian language – greetings and exhortations – should we generally discount its validity? (December 2002)

(1) Under the level of a 5th degree Master, no. (2) No. (3) I certainly would.

BENJAMIN CREME'S WORK WITH THE SPACE BROTHERS

How did you become involved with the work of the Space Brothers? (July/August 2004)

In the beginning of January 1959, I was contacted by one of the Masters of our Spiritual Hierarchy and my work began – I have talked and written about it elsewhere. The work was with the Space Brothers, the people using the UFOs, and my Master acted as the liaison between us, so to speak. To me, the two became identified; the fact of having read Adamski left me very open to the possibility, although I had not thought very much about it. But I was immediately introduced to the flying phenomena and I was part of a group, of which Adamski was one. To the outer world, we worked secretly, but to ourselves there was no secret – we recognized each other and we were part of a committee and did certain work which was assigned to us which was all to do with the UFO phenomenon.

In my experience, what we call UFOs, the flying saucers, come from the planets of our own system. Not from the Pleiades, or Sirius or somewhere outside our solar system, but from, mainly, Mars and Venus, although a few other planets like Jupiter and Mercury are involved. Practically all of the spacecraft are made on Mars, even the Venusian ones. They are Venusian in design, and they are quite distinct, different in design and technology, but they are actually constructed on Mars. And they are all constructed by thought.

What is one of the most important things you have learned from working with the Space Brothers? What was the purpose of your contact with the Space Brothers? (April 2010)

I learned how much the happenings and actions of people on Earth, if they affect the world as a whole, concern the Space Brothers. They are seriously and consistently working on a spiritual mission for Earth

In your conference talk [2009] you mentioned that the Space Brothers are gentle and subtle. (April 2010)

It is obvious by the way they have presented themselves through crop circles, crosses of light on buildings and so on, that they are capable of the most gentle type of approach. That is normally part of their way of doing it.

They do not want to infringe human free will or create havoc. They go about it very quietly, just showing you, if you have eyes to see and a mind to think with, that they have left their visiting card, clearly stating: "We are from space, the other planets of your system. We have come to help you. We are engaged in work on your behalf. Here is a sample of our work. We hope you like the 'drawing'."

We have to ask where the crop circles come from. They appear in the middle of fields in Wiltshire and elsewhere, enormous things. They cannot be made by human hands and yet there is nothing to show how they were done. They are actually done in a few seconds, however big they are. The plan has already been drawn up, the machinery is set, and as the craft moves for a few seconds over a piece of ground, the turning, crossing and bending of the grass of the crop takes place automatically as they guide the craft in. It has all been planned in advance so that the craft will not do anything else.

But it is quiet. Crops are seasonal and at the end of the season when the whole thing is cut down there is no sign of the crop circle. Some people say: "I have never seen a crop circle in my life. I know some people say there are circles, but I do not believe it." People can say that because the crops have all been cut down when they visit.

The Space Brothers work quietly. But when you work for the Space Brothers, you have to be dedicated to their work because they are without the ability to be tired! They are tireless in their devotion to helping Earth, and they expect those who work with them to be the same.

What have your experiences been regarding the Space Brothers? How did the Space Brothers' work lead to your work with the emergence of Maitreya? (April 2010)

I took part in the work of a group in London who claimed connection with at least three Space People – one Venusian and two from Mars. The information given by the Martians was severe and rather rigidly presented. That given by the Venusian was gentler in its presentation, less tough. This gave me an experience of the way they work. Most of the work they did through this group was the release of their energies through the group, like giving a Transmission. It was a transmission of energies out to the world, but was not called Transmission Meditation. It was not meditation. The people were just there and while they were there the space people sent their energies through them into the world.

That group changed its nature at a certain point and I was asked to withdraw from it, which I did. I was then approached by one of the Masters and the rest you know. I have been doing this work since that time. At first it was with and for the Space Brothers, and my Master acted as the liaison between me and them.

There are so many facets of the work with the Space Brothers that it is very difficult to do more than just give a tiny hint. They work with groups. I worked with a group of whom Adamski was a part. We only met outside the body. We did not meet in the physical body. We would not meet in a club or anything like that. Some of us knew each other on the outer plane but we did not meet as a group except out of the body. There we discussed. It is probably difficult for you to imagine what we would talk about. But I can just tell you this: we had plans that we discussed – what should be done and what could be done, what could not be done and why and so on. The longer one worked for the Space Brothers the more involved one got. I had a particular work to do also in connection with the actual spacecraft. I did not have a car at that time and had not learned to drive. I never felt any urge or need to drive. But the work I was doing with the Space Brothers, from their point of view, would be better served if I could drive, so I learned to drive a car.

I am afraid I cannot speak openly about the nature of my work with the Space Brothers but eventually it led to the work which I have been doing, preparing the way for the externalization of our Spiritual Hierarchy with Maitreya at its head.

THE INVISIBLE PERIL

by the Master —, through Benjamin Creme

If men were to see the state of the world as We, the Masters, see, they would be amazed, dumfounded and afraid, all at the same time. So far from the reality is man's view of conditions on Earth, and so lacking in judgment is he about future possibilities, that, without help, man would watch his planetary home languish and die.

As it is, planet Earth is in a sad and perilous condition while each day brings it nearer to the critical. Many voices have sounded warnings on global warming, and many views have been expressed, but even the most dire prophecy falls short of the calamity facing the world today. Few there are who see the immediacy of the threat and the urgency of the steps needed to counter it.

Great as is the peril posed by global warming, this, unfortunately, is not the greatest, or most hazardous, faced by man today. Did he but know it, man is engaged in a slow but steadily increasing intoxification of the race and of the lower kingdoms. Toxicity, pollutions, of all kinds, and in all fields, is now the greatest danger to men, animals and the Earth itself. All are poisoned and sick in their own way.

Unknown to men but evident to Us, the greatest harm sustained by men and planet in this sorry tale is caused by nuclear radiation. Men have gone far astray in the development of this most dangerous energetic source. Led astray by greed, and the false hope of vast profits, they have concentrated their experiments in 'taming' the most dangerous source of energy ever discovered by man, neglecting, meanwhile, a perfectly safe alternative use of the energy of the atom. Atomic fusion, cold and harmless, could be theirs from a simple isotope of water, everywhere available in the oceans, seas and rivers, and in every shower of rain.

Man must cease his 'toying with death'. Atomic fission is the result of the atomic bombs which destroyed Hiroshima and Nagasaki; which erupted in Chernobyl and causes, subtly, death and sickness today. It is "that which stands where it ought not" and which must be renounced by man if he would prosper further.

Earth scientists are confident that they have, indeed, tamed the monster, and can keep it under control. They do not realize that their instruments are crude indeed, that they measure only the lower aspects of nuclear radiation, that stretching above these dense-physical levels are levels finer and more dangerous to the health and well-being of all. But for the tireless efforts of our extra-planetary Brothers in assuaging this invisible peril in so far as the karmic law allows, our plight would be perilous indeed. Wake up, mankind!

(*Share International*, June 2006)

65

ETHERIC MATTER AND CURRENT SCIENCE

Why do our scientists say there are no humans on other planets?
(July/August 2004)

The people in physical bodies on Mars and Venus, Mercury, Jupiter and so on are not at the same level or vibration of physicality that we experience. We know only three aspects of the physical: solid physical, liquid physical and gaseous physical. Above gas there are still four further levels of physical matter, which so far have not been discovered on this planet. When they are discovered we will understand a great deal more about the nature and origin of disease, the purpose of life on this planet and of the reality of life on other planets.

The beings on Mars and Venus and the other planets are on the four higher levels of the physical. If you went to Mars or Venus you would see no one, but nevertheless they are in physical matter, and have bodies made of that subtle, finer physical matter to which we give the term 'etheric'. We ourselves have bodies of dense physical, liquid physical, gaseous physical and the four etheric physical planes – but we have not yet discovered the latter.

They have been demonstrated to exist by the great scientist and psychologist Wilhelm Reich, who was a colleague and one-time assistant of Freud. He died in an American prison in 1957. He was arrested for purporting to treat diseases with instruments which he claimed (correctly) attracted matter from the etheric planes, which he called 'orgone energy'. He saw it as one vast plane of orgone energy, which he saw, rightly, as being everywhere in the universe, substanding the outer solid physical plane. Esotericists understand the etheric plane as four planes, becoming finer and finer as they go higher. The fourth etheric is just above gas, and is invisible unless you have etheric vision. The reality of this etheric energy, 'orgone energy', was demonstrated palpably by him in various experiments. Nevertheless, he was arrested because he used an instrument he called the 'orgone accumulator', a box which accumulated the etheric energy of usually the two lower levels, and the fourth and the third etheric, to treat various diseases including cancer. In America that was deemed illegal. The Food and Drug Administration arrested him, refusing to allow him to prove his work, and he died in prison.

Unless one understands the reality of the etheric levels of energy as finer, subtler, levels of matter, one cannot begin to understand the UFO phenomenon, or the creation of crop circles – because they are all related.

How close are scientists to discovering the four levels of etheric matter? (March 2010)
Really quite close. They have already postulated something they call 'dark matter'. They know it is there but cannot pinpoint it. Their calculations show them that there is something they are missing. There is some material substance that is invisible. They cannot prove it but all their calculations point to the fact that such levels of matter exist. These are the etheric planes of matter. They only have to look up any esoteric journal to find out about the etheric. But they would rather make a cyclotron costing £20 billion, and spend years sending electrical currents through it, increasingly speeding it up to find out what this matter is. They could find out so easily if they would just open, for instance, *The Secret Doctrine* by H.P. Blavatsky.

Some scientists know about the findings of Wilhelm Reich, who discovered what he called the 'orgone' in 1939. The orgone is nothing other than the four etheric planes of matter. Reich saw them as one field of matter but it is actually one field divided into four planes, each one finer and finer. Some people have carried forward his experiments. At what level and how far that has reached in a world sense, I do not know. Many astronomers today are talking about dark matter. They know that it is something which all their theoretical experiments show to exist but which they have not yet proven to be other than an idea.

67

So dark matter is the same as orgone and the same as the etheric planes of matter. Relatively very soon scientists will either discover it for themselves or it will be given to them. Which it will be, I do not know.

You have previously mentioned that the Space Brothers are working with scientists in Russia and America. Are they merely impressing them mentally or are they working alongside them in the lab? Are the Space Brothers working with altruistic scientists or military scientists? (March 2010)

It is true that they are working to some extent with scientists in America and Russia. They are both impressing their minds and working with them in the laboratory. Are the Space Brothers working with altruistic scientists or military scientists? As a matter of fact, with both.

What must be done to get scientists to recognize the dangers of nuclear radiation that is threatening planet Earth? (March 2010)

Spell it out again and again. Write to the newspapers, write to television and radio. Talk to your local journalists and get it into local newspapers and it will go from there into the major newspapers. It will take Maitreya and what He has to say to convince our scientists of the limitations of their 'brilliant' minds. They understand a part and think it is the whole.

What do you see on the first etheric plane and how is it different from the second etheric plane? How is that different from the third etheric plane? What do you see on the fourth etheric plane? (March 2010)

It is like everything else. You see the level at which you are. Every expansion of consciousness, which initiation is, gives a greater and greater capacity for experiencing reality as it is. Everyone will see what they see depending on how developed their etheric vision is. To put it simply, and not necessarily exactly, the lower the etheric vision the grosser will be that which is seen on the etheric planes. The more developed the etheric vision, the more subtle will be its field of vision. It is also possible to skip a plane and to see subtle rather than grosser etheric matter.

More and more children will come into incarnation from now on who will have already developed some etheric vision. It is a development of the eye. When enough children are demonstrating that they can see what others do not see, the etheric planes will become known and accepted.

Physicists are continuing Einstein's search for a 'Theory of Everything', seeking to unify the four fundamental forces of the universe – the strong force, the weak force, gravity and electromagnetism. (1) Is there a unifying principle? (2) Is 'string theory' a fairly accurate way of understanding the universe? (3) How long do you think it will be before the etheric levels of existence are widely known and accepted as part of our physical reality, in particular, in the West? (June 2008)

(1) Yes. (2) Yes. (3) In about 30 years.

POLLUTION AND NUCLEAR RADIATION

One has heard recently in the news about the ITER (International Thermonuclear Experimental Reactor) project, which is a nuclear reactor, based on nuclear fusion. It will replace the actual reactors working on nuclear fission. It is a 500 megawatt reactor (fission reactors go up to 1,000 megawatts) but will only be operational in about 30-40 years.

It is said to be safer than a fission reactor. (1) Is this the case? To be functional these reactors require tremendous heats as opposed to cold nuclear fusion. (2) Isn't cold nuclear fusion the better solution or (3) does cold nuclear fusion produce too little energy as opposed to 'hot' nuclear fusion? (March 2004)

(1) Yes. (2) Yes. (3) No.

There may well be exper

many places in the world, but so far no one has come up with a device which in commercial terms is worthwhile developing. There is a process, still to be discovered, which is inexpensive and safe, using a simple isotope of water.

Also, and this is criminal, there are instances where a certain fusion process has been developed and bought by the nuclear fission authorities and is sitting on a shelf, or in a safe in that institution, awaiting development – which will never happen because it would interfere with the millions of dollars which are being generated for some people by nuclear fission.

There are also many plans for cars which do not need petrol which are sitting in the safes of the great automobile manufacturers until oil runs out.

Our planet Earth is limping, ailing, through space. From our misuse of resources, from the insane competition between the nations, we have rendered our planet sick. The restoration of the health of our planet must become our number one priority after the saving of the starving millions.

The worst pollution poisoning everything – the waters, the air, the rivers, seas – is nuclear radiation, which we cannot even see or measure. We build nuclear reactors around the world but our scientists cannot see the effects of their ignorant actions.

On 16 July 2007 a 6.8 magnitude earthquake rocked the world's largest nuclear plant at Kashiwazaki, Japan, causing a transformer fire and spills and leaks at the plant. (1) Was the nuclear leak in Japan worse than the government made out? (2) Was there any UFO activity over the area either before or after the damage caused by the recent quake? (September 2007)
(1) Yes. (2) Yes, both before and after.

I read in one of your books that nuclear fusion is safe and will produce unlimited energy. How close are scientists to doing this on a big enough scale so that all the world will benefit? (January/February 2008)

There are several approaches to nuclear fusion and some progress has been made by isolated scientists to develop this process. However there is one simple way which has not yet been discovered: using a simple isotope of water, everywhere available. If the will were there, and if a fraction of the billions spent on nuclear fission reactors were directed to the task, it would not be long until nuclear fusion became everywhere available. The continuing presence of the nuclear bomb makes politicians and scientists continue their misguided use of atomic fission. They fear to fall behind in a nuclear 'race'.

How great is the danger from nuclear weapons? (July/August 2009)

Humanity is the key. If we do not listen to Maitreya's advice for sharing, justice, peace, and right relationship, this Earth will cease to be. We either share or we die. We now have the most powerful weapon that has ever been devised, the nuclear weapon. Japan had two atomic bombs dropped on it at the end of the Second World War. Compared with the bombs of today, those were like toys, but they killed many thousands of people. Today, it is believed that nine nations (now 10 if we include North Korea) in the world have nuclear weapons. These are the official ones; there are actually 24 nations which have nuclear bombs, openly or otherwise. If these were used, it would be the end of life on planet Earth for millions and millions of years.

We have to get rid of nuclear radiation in all its aspects as soon as we possibly can.

If a nuclear reactor is built, but never operational (ie never turned on), (1) can it still pose a threat of polluting the environment and atmosphere? Likewise, (2) if a reactor is shut down, can it still pose a threat if idle or during the dismantling process? (3) If so, how serious a threat would it be? (October 2009)

(1) Yes. (2) Yes. (3) It depends on the skill in handling them.

In France there are anti-nuclear groups that say that 50 million people have died directly or indirectly from nuclear power and I think that includes pollution. Could your Master say whether that figure is correct? (January/February 2009)

I do not know how they come to that figure. How do they measure how many people have died as a result of nuclear radiation? Unless you are a Master it is impossible to gauge. My Master says that in the last three years, some 200,000 people have died in the world as a result of nuclear radiation at levels which are not known to affect people at all. It is a rough figure but not 50 million.

What is the significance of the Russian nuclear accident at Chernobyl in terms of the viability of nuclear power as a safe means of energy? (June 1986)

It is obvious that this unfortunate accident demonstrates, once again, how volatile and potentially dangerous is our present (fission) method of using nuclear energy. Significantly, the Russian scientists involved have said that the explosion and subsequent overheating of the fission rod occurred in a way which could not have been predicted from current scientific knowledge. If this is true, therefore, the same dangerous situation may well exist in every nuclear plant in the world. That being so, there is only one answer to the problem: the closing down of all nuclear plants and the abandonment of the current fission method of extracting energy from the atom. This would release the resources for full-scale research into the fusion process – already theoretically possible. Using a simple isotope from water, available everywhere, the fusion process of the future will give us unlimited energy for all our needs, safely.

Incidentally, my Master, commenting on the Chernobyl accident, said it was serious but that the radiation threat was not nearly so widespread or as dangerous as Western media had made out, nor were the numbers of people killed anywhere near the Western speculation. This has since been admitted by the American head of the International Atomic Energy Agency. My Master also said that within about a week after the accident the Space Brothers would begin neutralizing the worst concentration of nuclear radiation, up to the limits of karmic law. They had sought and received permission from the Lords of Karma to act on our behalf in this way.

*A UFO researcher, Robert Hastings, author of **UFO and Nukes: Extraordinary Encounters and Nuclear Weapons Sites** (published in 2008), related a number of incidents in an interview (**SI**, March 2010) where groups of nuclear missiles at launch facilities at Air Force Bases in the US malfunctioned simultaneously at a time when UFOs were sighted hovering over the missile silos. The ex-Air Force personnel Hastings interviewed seemed to think that the UFOs were deliberately demonstrating that they have the ability to interfere with the functioning of the nuclear missiles and the personnel who had experienced those malfunctions were ordered never to discuss those incidents.*

Can you confirm that the UFOs he mentioned, hovering over various nuclear sites, missile bases and power plants, were carrying out operations to 'mop up' some of the radiation leaking into the atmosphere? Or were they demonstrating their capabilities? (March 2010)

No. Their presence was observational. They were testing the strength of radiation coming from nuclear sites. The disablement was inadvertent. Many people have reported over the years that their cars have stalled or lights have gone out if there are UFOs in the vicinity. The energy of the spacecraft has an effect on the engines of the cars. It is common, but a transient experience.

In the same interview of Robert Hastings, he related reports involving the Chernobyl incident that "a globe, a spherical-shaped object was observed hovering over the shattered exploded reactor for a few seconds. Two crimson beams of light were seen to emanate from the globe down into the reactor itself". Was this UFO neutralizing the effects of the radiation? (March 2010)

In the case of Chernobyl, there was a deliberate intent to lower the destructive radiation over Russia and Europe, although they could not prevent the accident for karmic reasons.

SAVING THE PLANET

On a recent British television programme it was claimed that a large part of global warming is caused by the oceans, and is entirely natural. Would you please comment? (May 2007)

This is a very dangerous idea and widely believed by those who would gladly accept that we need do nothing to prevent or reduce our emissions of carbon gases which cause global warming. It is very important that we learn to cope not only with global warming but also with the complete changes that are taking place in the fabric of our planet. There are many scientists on both sides of this question, and the purveyors of oil are not slow to employ those who say there is nothing to worry about. According to the Masters, Who are the only people who can know with certainty, 80 per cent of the rise in temperature in the world is due to global warming caused by man. Twenty per cent is due to certain changes in the relation between the sun and the Earth, which Maitreya Himself has brought about, in part to draw our attention to the urgency of dealing with this danger to our planetary life.

Some scientists say that planting trees to combat climate change is a waste of time, since most forests don't have an overall effect

*on global temperature; and those farthest from the equator could
actually be making global warming worse. Whenever I travel by
plane I choose to make a contribution to a tree-planting project
to offset carbon emissions. Is this all a waste of time? Could you
please comment on this?* (January/February 2008)

My information is that this 'scientific' assertion is simply not
true. Equatorial forests do indeed have the greatest absorption
factor of carbon, but forests everywhere have at least a 30 per
cent absorption factor of carbon dioxide, which they exchange,
with a similar percentage of oxygen.

*Is recycling waste really helpful in combating climate change?
Some experts say it takes more energy to recycle than to just
incinerate.* (January/February 2008)

The aim of recycling is to economize on the use of basic
resources so on almost every occasion it is the way least
destructive of the planet's good.

*Is it worth doing all these little things like not using too much
water, turning off lights, using special light bulbs and so on, or
is that just a way of avoiding tackling the big problem?*
(January/February 2008)

The real problem is global and has to be tackled from a global
agreement to reduce drastically our demands on the world's
resources. Developed nations, in particular, will have to simplify
their way of life. This could be difficult to do for many people.
To start in the ways you suggest is a very good way to train
oneself from day to day. Look on these measures as good
training for the future.

*What do you think about carbon capture and storage technology
– to capture carbon dioxide and store it underground for long
periods?* (January/February 2009)

For thousands of years. The major problem in all these ideas is
the need to get rid of the waste. The use of nuclear energy itself

is not seen as a problem. The nuclear scientists do see a problem in the disposing of the waste produced in using nuclear energy – it is even dumped in the oceans, in steel and concrete canisters. It profoundly changes the ocean's ecology. It is bad enough at the present time and but for the work of the Space Brothers it would be infinitely worse.

The climate is being changed; the life of fish of all kinds is being modified, all due to the storage of nuclear radiation. All the waste they have is what they call 'small-scale nuclear radiation'. Well, it has nothing to do with the scale. If you put the waste in the sea, it is contaminated from the very beginning and they only have instruments that are able to read the radiation up to a certain point. Above that, they do not have the technology to measure it. So they assume that it is not relevant. But that is the most dangerous level of radiation, and they know nothing about it.

Carbon storage has a similar problem. They have to store it somewhere – somewhere it will do no harm. Well, where does it do no harm? Not in my backyard, I say and so does everyone else. The problem is that nowhere is safe. Where do you put carbon stored in canisters deep underground for thousands of years where it will do no harm? They do not know the harm it will do and they do not know when it will be broken into, broken open by the forces of the Earth itself in an earthquake, say, and released again.

It is always tackling a problem from the wrong end. We do not look for the cause and tackle that cause. What is causing this problem? What is causing global warming? If it is partly caused by the destruction of trees, then we have to stop cutting down our trees, especially the ancient primal forests of the world whose trees are great storers of carbon dioxide and pour oxygen into our atmosphere in return. Our atmosphere is becoming deoxidized and the carbon dioxide has nowhere to go, and so it creates global warming. But if we were not so profligate in our use of wood, we would cut out a great source of global warming.

We do not look for the cause because we do not like causes. They are to do with laws, as in cause and effect, and we do not like it. We prefer to be beyond the discipline of the Law. The modern mechanical mind never looks for the cause because it does not want to change its technology. We may say we cannot do without wood. But what the rich countries do is preserve their own hardwood and buy what they need from poorer countries, like Brazil, countries in Africa and elsewhere. These countries are then forced to cut down, or allow to be cut down, their ancient forests, which are absolutely essential to human life.

So if we want to know what to do about anything we look for the cause. And if we find it, we seek to remedy the cause. Everything is simple. We can build cyclotrons that are 23 kilometres long and take 20 years to build and cost billions of dollars. But if you ask an esotericist he will tell you the answers. For free. In a minute.

Biofuels are being heavily promoted as a viable alternative fuel source. But biofuels are cultivated at the expense of the local people, their crops, the forests and all animal and bird life in them, the air, the soil and water sources. It seems we are caught on the horns of a disastrous dilemma. Your suggestions or comments please. (December 2007)
This is another wrong decision by humanity, driven, as are most of our decisions today, by market forces (the forces of evil, as Maitreya calls them) in our eagerness to find an alternative to oil dependency. It will take Maitreya to point the way to sanity.

What is the most effective way of cleaning up pollution in the soil, often contaminated with cadmium, lead and many other chemicals? (December 2007)
For the ultimate, perfect, solution we must await the advice of the Masters, but there is much that we can do for ourselves,

above all, by ceasing to use the earth, the rivers and oceans as dustbins of our greedy urge for growth.

Have the ecologists really said that planet Earth has just 15 to 20 years left? Is that an exaggeration? (April 2008)
Not the ecologists but the Masters have said that we do not have 50 to 100 years (as many ecologists believe) but 15 to 20 years to rescue the planet before it reaches a stage in which the problems become irreversible.

How do we best fix and solve the ethical dilemma of both over-population and over-consumption to save the Earth for future Earthlings? (October 2008)
By sharing the world's resources.

(1) Could your Master express His opinion on a very difficult scientific issue, that accelerating green technology development as much as possible will not suffice to fend off the dangers of global warming, an opinion recently expressed by persons like science journalist Sharon Begley and eminent scientist James Lovelock? (2) If so, would he suggest the method of reducing agricultural waste to charcoal by burning it in a low-oxygen environment, thus sequestering the carbon that the plants took from the air as they grew in solid form? (3) Or would He agree with Freeman Dyson, one of the smartest people in the world, that we should stop worrying and that the problem will turn out as big a dud as did the Y2K computer code issue at the start of the millennium, thus reassuring persons like myself whose own opinion keeps fluctuating back and forth? (May 2009)
(1) Yes. There are other factors besides global warming, for example, deforestation. The loss of so many ancient trees has resulted in a huge oxygen loss which must be restored. (2) Yes, that is one thing we could do for a start. (3) No, that attitude from one of the "smartest" people in the world would end in total disaster.

*When your Master said that cities of the future will be more humanely designed and also lesser in population, was he referring to a reduction in global population, both rural and urban, and if so would this be caused by the same factors, whatever they are, that are responsible for declining populations in Russia, Japan, and some European countries? Or is a global decline in population inevitable for the reasons given by James Lovelock, author of **The Gaia Hypothesis**? Lovelock says that a global warming of at least 2 degrees Celsius is sure to happen due to greenhouse gases already in the atmosphere, where they will remain for hundreds of years, and that the net result will be that by the end of the century, our planet will only be able to support agricultural production sufficient for a population of about 1 billion people. (1) Is this prediction overly pessimistic, in your view? (2) Or is it accurate and as Lovelock says, not really gloomy, given that 1 billion people is plenty, whereas also, humanity has passed through far tighter demographic 'bottlenecks' in the distant past and will be far wiser and stronger for having to do so yet again?* (September 2009)

If we were to do little or nothing to overcome global warming to some degree, Mr Lovelock's projection would quite possibly be accurate although global warming will at the same time make possible a huge area for cultivation in the sub-arctic regions of northern Europe, Russia and Canada which could produce enormous amounts of food for the world. In any case, it is likely that Mr Lovelock has not heard about the presence of Maitreya and of His coming emergence. If we respond, Maitreya and His group of Masters know what needs to be done to limit and overcome global warming. My Master has stated that this world can comfortably sustain and nourish about 4.5 billion people, and eventually the population of the Earth will be that, not by starvation or lack of food but by natural social control of the sex function and a more just social life and care for all groups. For example, the huge families of people in the poorest countries are governed by the need for support of parents in old age. They have many children because they know that most of them will die before they themselves do. It is their form of insurance for old age. When sharing and justice are realities in the world, this ignominy will change and the population will drop naturally.

THE 'STAR' HERALDING MAITREYA'S EMERGENCE

On 12 December 2008 Share International Foundation issued a press release announcing that very soon will appear a "star like luminary" heralding the first appearance of Maitreya on US television. The 'star' was first seen around Christmas 2008 in Norway and soon after throughout the world. This will continue until the Day of Declaration.

The 'star' is one of four gigantic spacecraft placed in our skies to the north, south, east and west so that they can be seen throughout the world.

MAITREYA'S FIRST INTERVIEW
by the Master —, through Benjamin Creme

In the very near future, people everywhere will have the opportunity to witness an extraordinary and significant sign, the like of which has been manifested only once before, at the birth of Jesus. Then, according to Christian teaching, a star appeared in the heavens and led three wise men from the East to the birthplace of Jesus. Soon, once again, a star-like luminary of brilliant power will be seen around the world. What does this mean? How is it possible?

The answer lies in the fact that this mysterious event is a sign, and heralds the beginning of Maitreya's open mission. Soon after the sign appears in our skies, Maitreya will give His first media interview on American television.

On that open, public occasion, still unannounced as Maitreya, the World Teacher will present His views on the economic and financial chaos which now grips the world. He will explain its origins and final outcome, and present, to some extent, His recipe for amelioration of the present heavy burden on the poor of the world. Thus He will prepare the way for a more detailed and specific announcement of His ideas.

How will viewers respond? They will not know His background or status. Will they listen to and consider His words? It is too soon to know exactly but the following may be said: never before will they have seen or heard Maitreya speak. Nor, while listening, will they have experienced His unique energy, heart to heart. Also, this is a unique time in history with whole nations stunned and apprehensive for the future. Therefore it can be assumed that many who hear His words will be open and eager to hear more. It is not for nothing that Maitreya has waited patiently for this moment to enter the public world; America, for one, would not have responded sooner. Now, for the first time in many years, a new Administration has to cope with financial chaos, unemployment and social unrest on a massive scale. The moment of truth for America and the world has arrived.

Not alone in America but worldwide, people are awakening to the need for and the possibility of change. The politicians and economists call the present situation a 'downturn' and a 'recession'. In truth, we are witnessing the last stumbling steps of the old order. Millions are becoming aware that unbridled competition and greed are not the safest path for men, that such materialistic doctrines create a 'slippery slope' for the unwary, and, eventually, the international crisis we have today.

Of course, many people of burgeoning wealth stand clear of the present loss of confidence in the ways which have made them rich, and think it only 'a matter of time' until we are back on course and thriving again.

Will they heed Maitreya and recognize the sense of His argument? Lost in their arrogance and self-esteem, possibly not. However, many are less sanguine about a return to the status quo. Many have suffered painful losses and have lost faith in the old methods. The peoples of the nations are ripe and ready for change. They call out for change and a more meaningful life.

Maitreya will remind men of the essentials without which there is no future for man: Justice and Peace. And the only way to both is through sharing.

(*Share International*, January/February 2009)

[Note: On 14 January 2010, Benjamin Creme announced at his public lecture at Friends House, London, that Maitreya had given His first interview on American television, and that millions had heard Him speak both on television and the internet.]

THE 'STAR' HERALDING MAITREYA'S EMERGENCE

What can we do to make Maitreya's emergence sooner and when approximately will He emerge? (October 2008)

My information is that He is emerging very, very soon – even by our standards. I have been told for over 30 years that He is emerging 'soon', but that is by the Masters' standards of time. They work in 2,000-year cycles, so a few years to the Masters is just like a Sunday afternoon.

Maitreya's emergence is based on certain laws, above all the laws governing our free will. At any time since 1982 He could have been invoked by humanity performing just a few actions which would have allowed Him to come forward.

At a press conference in May 1982 I talked to almost a hundred journalists from all the major networks of the USA plus the BBC, and revealed Maitreya's exact whereabouts – the Asian community of London, a fact that I had known for some years, but was not allowed to divulge until then. I invited the journalists to come to London and to go through the motions of looking for Maitreya. They did not have to find Him; they could not find Him without His help. But if one or two or three journalists of repute, and therefore with clout, would come to London and simply go through the motions of looking for Him, Maitreya would come forward to them. And nobody did anything.

So Maitreya had to take the long, slow path out into the world, which has taken over 30 years because humanity was not ready or did not make the media act. The media would not act unless they were pushed by humanity, and so nothing was done.

It has taken time for the events themselves like the stock-exchange crash, the banking crash to take place; the economic bubbles are bursting, as you well know, not only in the USA but in Europe and elsewhere in the world. Maitreya made that prediction in 1988. He said the collapse would take place and would begin in Japan. It did begin in Japan in 1989 when the Nikkei average fell from 40,000 points to 7,000 points and remained at about 7,000 to 10,000 for a decade or more.

The timing of Maitreya's emergence is up to humanity. If we do not act, Maitreya cannot act. There are laws governing an Avatar of such a stature as Maitreya. He cannot simply come in when you or I would like, or even when He would like.

What clues will we get that Maitreya is really emerging? (November 2008)
When Maitreya is about to step forward people will see a huge, bright, shining star, visible to everyone. I may not tell you what He will look like, not because it is a game but because it is important that you believe in what he is saying. It doesn't matter if you don't think He is Maitreya. If you see a man who is talking about sharing, justice and freedom for everyone, and a complete change in the world's relationships, then you might think: "Maybe that's Maitreya?"

Maitreya is not the only one talking about freedom and justice, and I am not the only one saying these things either. I am the only one relating it to Maitreya, but people have been talking about these ideas for years.

*At the birth of Jesus a large bright star appeared, leading the
'three wise men' to Him. More recently, one week before
Maitreya miraculously appeared in Nairobi in June 1988, Job
Mutungi reported in the Kenya Times that a "big bright star was
sighted above the city". (1) Were they really stars, and if not
what were they? (2) Does this happen with the advent of every
new Teacher?* (April 1996)

(1) They were spacecraft. (2) No.

*(1) Were there really historically genuine figures known as the
'three wise men'? (2) Who were they? (3) Why were they looking
for Jesus?* (January/February 2009)

(1) Yes. (2) They were Masters. (3) They were not "looking for"
Jesus. They came to pay their respects to the One Who would be
overshadowed by the Christ.

*(1) Is the new 'star' the return of the star of Bethlehem or the
"sign of the Son of Man" as prophesied by Jesus? (2) Are all
the things that have been happening in the recent past signs of
Him appearing soon? (3) How do you explain the Bible's
prophecy in Matthew 24:29-31, where Jesus says He will come
"on the clouds of heaven with power and great glory"? And the
scripture that says: "'And the Lord, whom you seek, will
suddenly come to His temple, even the Messenger of the
covenant, in whom you delight. Behold, He is coming', says the
Lord of Hosts." (Malachi 3:1) This is plainly talking about a
real temple in Israel (to me, at least). The problem is that the
Jewish people have not rebuilt the ancient temple of Solomon.
This prophecy is yet to be fulfilled. (4) How do you see this
happening?* (July/August 2009)

(1) The 'star' is, symbolically, the sign of the Son of Man and
heralds the first appearance of Maitreya, the World Teacher, on
US television, interviewed not as Maitreya, but as an ordinary
man. (2) Yes. (3) Maitreya descended from His retreat in the
high Himalaya on 8 July 1977, stayed some days in Pakistan,

then came from Karachi to London, UK, on 19 July 1977, by aeroplane, thus "coming in the clouds" which all can do today. (4) The 'temple' referred to in this symbolic text refers to the 'temple of truth'. Maitreya has said: "I am the Architect only of the Plan. You, My brothers, are the willing builders of the Temple of Truth" – a purified and cleansed humanity living in right human relationship.

I am confused about the connection between Maitreya and beings from other planets, eg the large spaceships that are appearing as the 'star'. What is the connection between Maitreya and these Beings? Why would they be involved in His coming? (October 2009)

We are all of us living in the same solar system that works as a unitary system. The public may not generally know about, or believe in, the reality of life on other planets of our system but the Hierarchies of all the planets are in contact. There is indeed a kind of Interplanetary Parliament representing all the planets. The Space Brothers are here to help the people of Earth to overcome the difficulties which our own ignorance has brought about, and to work with Maitreya, and our Spiritual Hierarchy as a whole, in the work of salvage.

Do the four 'stars' serve other functions besides heralding Maitreya's emergence? (March 2010)

Yes, they will also represent the fact of the Space Brothers – that is, when it becomes known that they are not actually 'stars', because stars are millions of miles away and these are 'star-like luminaries' in our atmosphere. So what are they? They are really spacecraft, and have come from different planets to take on the job of being a herald for Maitreya's emergence – just as one did 2,000 years ago at the birth of Jesus, when a spacecraft was sent to guide three Masters to Bethlehem. This is a repetition of that event, only now not only 'three wise men' but the whole of humanity who will know about this.

86

The fact that we were able to forecast the appearance of the 'stars' [12 December 2008] demonstrates that this information is correct. They began to be seen soon after Christmas 2008 and are now seen by people all over the world. They heralded Maitreya's first appearance on television.

When enough people are responding to Maitreya's teaching they will call on Him to speak to the whole world through the linked television networks. Only then will He reveal His true status. Maitreya will be on worldwide television so that for the first time everyone throughout the world will be able to see him. That is why it says in the Bible: "And all eyes will see Him." It takes television to make that possible.

The coming of the 'star' is a herald. It is a symbolic re-enactment of that happening 2,000 years ago to convince those who are ready to be convinced, who are open-minded enough to see it as symbolic, and prepare them for what is going to happen, the coming out into the world of the Christ, the World Teacher, but this time known worldwide.

When the Christ came last time, He was not really known as the Christ. He came to the Jews through Jesus as the Jewish Messiah. They were expecting the Messiah. When Jesus came he was not recognized even as the Messiah except by a very small group of people. Around him were only 12 disciples, a wider group of about 75 not-so-close disciples and about 500 people who were interested outsiders. That was the sum total. It hardly seemed like the coming of the Christ to the world, which in fact it was.

The last three years of Jesus' life, which he spent being the vehicle for the Christ, overshadowed by Maitreya, changed the face of the world. We have now come to the end of that phase. We are entering a new phase in which the Christ Himself comes openly into the world for all humanity.

THE RESTORATION OF THE WORLD

by the Master —, through Benjamin Creme

From almost every point of view the situation facing men everywhere grows daily more painful. The economic chaos resulting from years of unlicensed greed and heartless competition lays waste the honest toil and aspiration of countless millions. On the whole, the men of money go blithely on, their treasure intact, while men and women in every country face joblessness, poverty and fear. More accurate readings of climatic changes show men how close this planet is to irreversible calamity, and alarm bells sound loudly on many political fronts, raising to new levels the factor of stress.

How much more of this tension can humanity bear? For how long will men accept, mildly, their fate? Desperate men do desperate deeds and already in their minds, if not yet in their actions, many contemplate revolution.

Behind the scenes, Maitreya watches carefully these happenings, and gives succour wherever the Law allows. He waits, patiently, for the build-up of response to the sign of His Emergence, the "star-like luminary of brilliant power" on which many now gaze in wonder and even love.

What is desired is some measure of public debate about the significance or meaning of the Star, thus signifying the emergence of Maitreya, the World Teacher. The greater and more public the discussion, the more does it prepare the way for Maitreya's entry. Soon there will be no gainsaying. Very soon, Venus will move beyond the sight of men and so leave the platform of the heavens open to the Star. Then there will be no doubt that the Star is there for all to see.

If sufficient discussion can be fostered on the various media and internet it will not be long until men see and hear Maitreya speak. He will not be so called, that men can judge His ideas rather than His status.

As the economic crisis deepens, a singular reaction is appearing in many countries: alongside the fear, bravado and growing despair is a new understanding of the reasons for the crash – the greed and competitive spirit at the centre of our systems and, therefore, the need for sharing. Of themselves, many are awakening to this basic truth and see sharing as the answer to injustice and war. Thus are many ready for Maitreya's Call. This realization will grow as the crisis bites deeper and deeper into the shaky fabric of the outworn forms and structures that no longer work, can never be made to work for long.

When Maitreya speaks, He will show that this is so, that the world is ready for the adoption of new and better forms, based on the true needs of the peoples everywhere. His is the task to focus and strengthen this growing realization of the oneness and unity of men, of their mutual dependence and awakening divinity. Thus will Maitreya and humanity work together for the restoration of this world.

(*Share International*, April 2009)

MAKING KNOWN THE 'STAR'

For more than 20 years Maitreya's public emergence did not take place because there had to be a worldwide stock-market crash first. Maitreya forecast a crash in 1988. Finally there is a stock-market crash, and people around the world now can see the need for change that Maitreya calls for. Still there is no public emergence. Now there is a 'star' in the sky heralding his appearance, but there has to be a public debate about the meaning of the 'star' before his emergence can take place. I don't understand why there seems to be a new condition now for Maitreya's emergence. Can you explain why this is happening? (May 2009)

As you say, Maitreya did indeed forecast, in mid-1988, a world stock-market crash which He said would begin in Japan. In 1989 the Nikkei stood at 40,000 points. It suddenly collapsed to 7,000 points. Today it hovers around 10,000 points. Maitreya called the Japanese prosperity up till 1989 "a 'bubble' which inevitably would burst". This was followed by the collapse of the markets in the countries of the Pacific rim: Thailand, Malaysia, Hong Kong, Singapore, Indonesia. Then the markets collapsed in Russia, Brazil, Mexico and Argentina. America and Europe have survived a series of 'near-miss' collapses until the latest debacle. Do you really imagine that Maitreya can emerge the very next day? What He has given is a "star-like luminary of brilliant power" as a Sign, a Herald of His Return. He desires that there should be open discussion on media to create a general expectation of His Emergence. I have not said that His Emergence depends on that. It does not, but obviously it would alert millions to what is happening. You know about and, impatiently, expect to see and hear Maitreya but billions of people do not. Do they not also have the right to know? What better way to tell them about Maitreya and, at the same time, affirm the reality of the Space Brothers and their spaceships, the so-called UFOs?

People know nothing of the hugeness of this enterprise, nor of the laws which govern it. They desire something and are impatient to experience their desire fulfilled. But what do they do to help to bring it about? Generally, little or nothing. As Maitreya says: "Nothing happens by itself. Man must act and implement his will."

My colleagues and I have strained every nerve and sinew for many years making this information known. We do not put a date on Maitreya's appearance; we know He is here and that He will emerge openly at the earliest possible moment.

I was at your London lecture on 23 April 2009 and you spoke very urgently about the need to get the existence of the 'star' into media outlets (radio, television, the internet, etc), so that there would be an open public discussion/debate about its meaning. Why is that so important? (May 2009)

Maitreya desires as much public discussion as possible otherwise the function of the 'star' in heralding His approach is lost.

In our approach to the public and the media, should we speak more about the 'star' and the Space Brothers, in relation to the emergence of Maitreya? (April 2010)

As a member of this group, there is no difference in talking about the 'star' or about the reappearance of the Christ and the Masters of Wisdom. They are part of the same process. It is not one or the other; it is all part of a whole. It is the latest phase in a process that has gone on for years, by which Maitreya and the group of Masters who are coming with Him re-enter openly the modern world. They have already been in position in the world for years. This is a new phase and the 'star' is there as a herald for this process of working openly, reaching humanity through radio and television.

The 'star', of course, is not a star. It is one of 4 enormous spacecraft. The 'usual', 'everyday' scout craft UFOs are only about 25 to 30 feet in diameter, which is big but not all that big. The 'star' is gigantic, the size of five football fields put together.

If the reality of the 'star' can be presented to the public it does two things: it is a herald for Maitreya's advent in the physical, everyday world, and is also proof of the reality of the Space Brothers. Those 'stars' must have been made somewhere. I cannot prove to anyone that they were made on Mars and Venus, but that is my information, and I present it to anyone who wants to know. These two important things come together in this story: Maitreya's approach to the public beginning with His coming on television in the very near future (although unannounced as Maitreya) and also the knowledge of 'flying saucers' as a reality. You cannot talk about one without talking about the other.

How much energy should the group put into making the 'star' known to the media and to astronomers? (April 2010)

As much energy as you have. To make known the 'star' is to make known Maitreya. They are not separate. We only talk about the 'star' because it relates to Maitreya. The 'star' is only there because of Maitreya.

Creating differences in approach in making known Maitreya's presence or talking about the 'star' is not very useful. It is all one. The more you make known about the 'star', the more you make known about Maitreya. You cannot talk about them separately. The 'star' has no real meaning separately.

People are apt to think of the 'star' in terms of its UFO identity and therefore to do with flying saucers rather than with Maitreya. But it is a herald of Maitreya's coming. At the same time, it cannot be a herald and known as the herald for Maitreya without being known as an extraordinary kind of UFO.

It brings into people's consciousness the fact of the reality of UFOs, and the identity of the work of UFOs with the work of Hierarchy – that there is one big Hierarchy in the solar system. Each planet has its own individual Hierarchy as part of the inter-related work of all the planets working together at the behest of the Solar Logos. So you should not compartmentalize this work in your mind. It is all part of one whole.

What would be the best way to bring the 'star' to the attention of the media? (April 2010)

I will leave that to you. Every person in every group has ideas – see what works for you. Do not expect too much from the media, but that should not put you off approaching them. When you do approach the media, they may consult either astronomers from an observatory or some amateur who thinks he knows all about the heavens. They will say: "Thank you very much. We have our information on it. It was only Jupiter or Venus or Sirius or some other luminary."

The media want the reappearance of the Christ and all that pertains to it to be put into their lap. Everything about it is just out there and they only have to look up and see Maitreya, the Master Jesus and all the other Masters, and the 'star' just in front of their head. They want everything on a plate.

The thing to remember is that we see the 'star' in our own atmosphere. It is only a few thousand feet away. When we look at aeroplanes, they are about 30,000-35,000 feet up. We cannot touch them, but you do not feel that they are from outer space, you do not think of them as stars or planets. You know they are aeroplanes. In the same way, by its gyrations, its changing colours, its erratic movements, the 'star' presents itself very much as occurring in our atmosphere. When you see the 'star' you get no impression that it is millions of miles away like the stars. But you never think that the stars are up there just above your head. The 'star' is so much part of our sky that it is obvious that it is not a star or planet. It is something else. In fact, it is an enormous spacecraft.

The primary problem we have had in contacting the media and astronomers is that the 'star' has typically not been seen stationary sufficiently long enough to direct their attention to it. Do you know if this is likely to change anytime soon? (April 2010)
You mean that you will be given information about when a 'star' is going to appear and be stationary there, for instance at 7pm on Tuesday week? This kind of information is impossible to give.

You take your chance with seeing it. Those who do not see the 'star' have just not put in the time to look for it. The 'star' is there. It is not there all the time because it cannot be. There are four 'stars', not 104, and they have to replenish their batteries. That means being out of commission for a given number of hours, and then they can be active for another given number of hours. They are not appearing continuously so that every time you look up and it is clear you can see a 'star'. It is not like that.

There is a potential problem when contacting the media and astronomers when the 'star' is in the vicinity of a known celestial object (Venus or Jupiter, for example). This affects their acceptance of the phenomenon. Will this situation clarify with time? (April 2010)

No, I do not think it will. This is the age-old response of experts or anyone in authority. Whatever comes within the range of their particular discipline comes also within the range of their inhibitions, their credibility, antagonisms, predilections and their sense of knowing everything in their own discipline.

You must remember that the idea of flying saucers has been debunked by most countries in the world through the world's media. The media have shown their reluctance to make any clear-cut, unbiased investigation of this phenomenon for over 60 years. Nothing makes them change their approach today.

More people than ever before believe in the existence of UFOs. But they have been debunked by the media for over 60 years, so to expect an open minded approach to the 'star' by people in authority, to expect astronomers to give credence to this phenomenon, I will not say is foolish, but it would be approaching the miraculous.

The media are not on your side. It is a struggle to make it known. But that does not mean you should give in or get aggressive. You should just plough on presenting information to the media. Already unofficial channels like YouTube are filled with stories of the 'star', some under the name Maitreya's 'Star', others under the name of What is this Amazing Object? Is it a UFO?

That is what we want to get across to the media. It does not have to be mainstream media in the first place. However, there was a report on CNN in Texas, in the very early weeks of the appearance of the 'star', when someone photographed it and sent the video in. They showed the video on television and I saw it myself on YouTube. It was quite clearly the 'star'. They did not know what it was, but the woman presenter was thrilled with it. She was very congratulatory to the man who made the video of this extraordinary object. There have been other media coverage since that time but they have never been followed up. So it is possible to get the media to cover this story, but not at will.

Thanks for all of the great work that you have done so gracefully for so many years. I have one question that has been gnawing at my mind for several weeks: why have you been calling the light in the sky 'the star', while some of your regular readers know it is one or more UFOs?

It seems that many people would quickly become very confused by your references to 'the star', especially after they look at the photographs (and accompanying text) on the Share International website that clearly indicates that it appears and disappears in a wide variety of different locations, colours and forms, and that it moves around randomly (unlike any other star) like a spacecraft might.

To my mind calling it a' star' makes it all too tempting for the public (including all those who are open to UFOs), to dismiss the story as baloney. So, why not cut out the pretence and call it a UFO? (May 2009)

There is no pretence. Knowing the nature of the 'star' as four gigantic spaceships from several planets of our System, I had great difficulty in deciding just how to present it to the general public and media. I decided to follow my Master's example. He had called it a "star-like luminary of brilliant power", and related it to the 'star' which led the 'three wise men' to the birthplace of Jesus. Some of us know that that 'star' was a spacecraft too, but it is accepted by millions as a miracle star.

It was just before Christmas so I called it a 'Christmas star', sure that that would be more interesting and magnetic than a prediction about a UFO. In Britain at least, people are much more sceptical of UFOs than in the USA, for example. Of course, at each lecture I make it clear that what looks like a star is, in fact, one of four huge spacecraft. In a lecture, one has time and opportunity to enlarge on the subject and the meaning and purpose of the phenomenon. In a press release or advertisement one is limited by space and the need to be succinct. The result from the public has been encouraging – eager and excited and amazed by the sheer beauty of the spectacle. The response of the media has been muted, as if there were an embargo on mentioning something so important as the herald of the Christ. However, it could be that media interest is starting now.

BEHAVIOUR OF THE 'STAR'

Does the 'star' change position and colour in such a subtle way so that it is gentle enough to alert people but not to frighten them? (April 2010)

Yes, precisely. That is the way the Space Brothers behave and the way they make crop circles, for example. They want to contact the Earth. They want to allow people to understand what they are doing, who they are and where they come from, but they know all the glamours of humanity. They know how easily we become afraid. They witness the fear in people. Very often when they come down in the night, people walking along a country path might come upon a saucer already landed and when they see it they are so terrified that they run. This happens over and over again throughout the world. It is due to the fact they have been portrayed so adversely by government agencies and films.

The Space Brothers do not want to frighten us. They have work to do. They would like us to know and acknowledge it and to know consciously what is happening, but they know they have to step warily. So they do their work 'privately', in such a way that we can make up our own mind. In this way our free will is left intact. They never infringe human free will.

Why does the 'star', the spaceship, look so much like Jupiter, and why is it to be found at the moment near Jupiter? What is the point if the purpose is to draw attention to it? Why is it close to Jupiter? (April 2010)

It is not close to Jupiter. Jupiter is on a line of motion. It cannot alter its course. It is drawn around the sun. It is on its own elliptic which it cannot alter. But the 'star' does not have to obey that astronomical reality. It is a free agent, and can go higher or lower, as it likes.

So it is not true to say the 'stars' behave like Jupiter. They do not behave like any planet. Their movements can be erratic. They appear bigger, then smaller; they disappear, then come back; they change colour, rotate, move up and down or sideways. Planets do not change colour. They have their colour and that remains the same. The light emitted from a planet is the same all the time, as far we are concerned. But with the 'star', there is a sequence of colours. It changes from one to another through the whole gamut of the rainbow.

When Venus was high in the sky everyone thought the 'star' was Venus. Now that Venus is low, Jupiter has taken its place. Many people who would believe, and say they believe, that the story of Maitreya's return to the world is the closest thing to their heart, find it very difficult to believe about the 'star'.

I have seen it for myself that even when some people see things with their own eyes, they still don't believe the evidence because that evidence sits very uncomfortably with their fear. People have a fear of this whole phenomenon, and that is what prevents even people who really believe about Maitreya from having the same conviction about the 'star'. They are put off by other people who they think know better, by being told: "Oh, it is probably Venus, Jupiter or Sirius, or some other large luminary in the sky."

What's the best way to see the 'star'? (April 2010)

The best way is for everyone to get a tripod and a good quality camera with a zoom lens so that you can zoom right into the 'star'. If you zoom right into Mars, Jupiter, Venus or whichever planet, you would still see just the planet. But if you zoom into the 'star' of Maitreya, the spaceship, you see it as a spaceship – usually like a rounded diamond shape.

Perhaps we could learn to use our intuition, or otherwise factual information, so that we know it is the 'star'. When we are sure of our information we can present it to the public or the media. (April 2010)

I have spelled it out. I have described everything the 'star' does that planets and stars absolutely do not do. If you see an object moving about the sky, going in and out, rotating or changing colour, you know it is not Jupiter or Venus. It really is a matter of common sense. People have a mystical idea about the 'star', but there is nothing mystical about it.

Maitreya wants the 'star' to be known throughout the world and prepare the way for Him, so people think it should show every minute of the day and night. People take for granted that it should be as they expect when they do not know what can be done. How often does this phenomenon occur? It has been 2,000 years since anything like this event occurred, and then it was on a tiny scale, one spacecraft.

This is a colossal enterprise. These huge spacecraft have a propulsion system that needs to be charged directly from the sun. For some hours each of them goes higher in the atmosphere so that they are nearer the sun and can recharge the batteries. That means they cannot be seen all the time. They have so many hours of activity and so many hours of non-activity. Why do people imagine that there is a better way of doing things than the way the Hierarchy of Masters do them? The Masters are the most advanced beings on planet Earth. Why should you assume that you have a better understanding of what needs to be done for the purpose of making known the 'star', and therefore about Maitreya, than Maitreya Himself does?

Are governments or media actively suppressing information about the 'star'? (April 2010)
Governments are not suppressing information about the 'star', but some media definitely are. The attitude of the media is that there is not sufficient demand or sufficient noise about it. They do not have enough information. They would like to send out their cameramen to photograph it, if only they knew where it would be in advance. Likewise, if I had told them when Maitreya was coming on a particular programme they would all be there with their cameras. They would assess whether that person could be Maitreya or not, and in the end they would not know. So unlike is Maitreya to their idea of the Christ that they would probably just ignore that person as a possible Maitreya or Christ.

When He came to the office of the BBC, they rejected Him. He was in the office of the BBC in around 1986. He had interviews with the Director-General and colleagues. They were shown the last hours of Jesus on the cross as if they were there. They witnessed this. They saw it with their own eyes. They experienced it. They saw the agony, the blood, the people, all of that.

The Master Jesus was asked by Maitreya to come into the office and He came, so that they met the Master Jesus as well. They were asked and agreed to mount a big press conference at which Maitreya would appear, talk to the journalists and answer all their questions.

But they did nothing about it. Instead, they made the information known to the Queen who, as head of church and state, they thought should be the first to know. They probably knew what the Queen would do, which was to call on her advisors in the church, the Archbishop of Canterbury and the

Bishops. They met and their view was that there was no way that this could be the Christ without their knowing.

So there was a complete embargo on this information. That is why Maitreya had to take this long slow way round of nearly 30 years, working behind the scenes, gradually preparing the way and making it possible to come out now when a window of opportunity has been created with the collapse of the world's economy, as He prophesied in 1988.

Sometimes people in the group ask for the 'star' to appear, and it does, and sometimes people ask for the 'star' to appear and it does not. Why does it show up sometimes and not others? Should we be asking for the 'star' to appear? (April 2010)
Personally I do not think you should be asking for the 'star' to appear. You either believe it is there and let it be, and if you see it, fine; if you do not see it, it is also fine. Not everyone in all of the groups sees the 'star', and it is not that important for you to see it. But it is important that enough people see it and can respond to it in a way that makes the media take it seriously. The more that it is talked about in the media, the more it prepares the way for Maitreya, because the 'star' and Maitreya's emergence are interconnected.

Do not make it a personal thing. I find as I go from group to group, almost every individual is full of desire to see the 'star'. "Why am I not the seeing the 'star'? I know some people see it. Are they just lucky? What have I not done that does not let me see it? I know some people who think they have the 'star' at the end of a wire and can make it do anything they like. And I cannot see one."

This is personalizing it. It is nothing to do with the personalities of the groups.

MAITREYA'S LIGHT-SHIP

What does Maitreya need His light-ship for? What does He use it for? (April 2010)

Maitreya has a light-ship, which is often seen as a red or orange-red ball, and it holds quite a few people. He uses it to get about and to show people events ahead of their taking place.

Maitreya lives in a variety of temples in London, spends a few years in each, trains the swamis and then sends them out to teach all over the world. While He is doing this He often takes people in His light-ship.

The Masters see events before they happen. They know these events are going to precipitate down onto the physical plane and be something you read about in the newspapers in two days' time, for example. Maitreya takes people up and shows them the event happening at that highest level, and has done this over and over again – catastrophes, like the blowing up of oil rigs, or the ending of a hijacking on a plane.

On one particular occasion there were three or four terrorists from North Africa who had hijacked a plane with about 60 people on board, so they had 60 hostages. They kept flying from place to place and no one would let them land for long. They would get more fuel to go somewhere else, but no one would have them in their country. This went on for a couple of days. The world's media covered the story day by day. The group threatened to kill the hostages one by one until their needs were met. They did in fact kill one man and threw the body out of the plane. In the end, they landed in Algeria, I believe, and were given asylum there. But they were still vicious and, at first, pretty sure that they were going to go ahead with killing all the hostages, if necessary.

Maitreya took a group of people in His light-ship to Algeria, up above the airfield where they could see the plane. Maitreya homed in on the people on the ground so those in the light-ship could see them as if they were looking through a telescope. They could see the hijackers' expressions. They were very angry and agitated because things were not going their way. By then, they did not want to go through with the process of killing all the hostages. At the same time, they thought it was the only way to get what they wanted – asylum with impunity, free from any harm.

Maitreya said to the people in His light-ship: "Now watch them. They are beginning to change in their minds. There is a change in their resolve." The people in the craft watched them. The hijackers began to be very divided and Maitreya said: "They are wondering whether it is worth it. They are thinking: 'I do not know how long we can put up with this.'" Maitreya said: "Now watch," and He pointed His finger at the leader and moved it slightly.

Maitreya used a certain amount of energy from Himself, through His finger, and touched the soul, the heart centre in the right side of the chest, just touched it enough so it did not infringe their free will: they had to be already on the point of giving up. They were so confused that they were beginning to argue angrily among themselves. Maitreya saw that they were near to giving up. He just made certain that it happened. But he would not have done it until they were ready; inside, they had already begun to give up.

On the ground, the leader smiled and then they all smiled and did a little dance together holding each other by the shoulders. They danced around like that on the plane. Then they threw away their weapons and the whole thing was over. It is for this sort of thing that Maitreya uses His light-ship, to take people to events before they happen.

One of my first great experiences when Maitreya told me that I would have work to do in His coming out into the world, if I accepted it, was that I was given a view of how the Masters see reality. I was in a great sphere of light. In that light, if I turned my eyes to the right I could see all the events of the past, which were still taking place, some I recognized as historical events. If I turned my eyes to the left, I saw the events of the future, as if they were already taking place in front of me. On that highest level they were already taking place but had not yet precipitated downward through the planes onto the dense-physical plane. So they were not yet events but would become events.

I saw myself talking to crowds of people. I saw crowds running around the streets crying with joy that the Christ had returned and so on. It was extraordinary – as you will see after the Day of Declaration. For weeks afterwards, people will be thrilled through and through. I could see all of this. It has already happened, but not yet on the physical plane. We have to understand there is no past, present or future. There is only this moment now. That is all there is. This exact moment is reality.

Our distorted vision, our illusionary makeup makes us think of the past and the future, but essentially there is only now. That is how the Masters see reality. That is why it is so difficult for the Masters to give to any event a correct, accurate date, in our terms and meaning of date.

Many people are disappointed that Maitreya seems to delay His coming out. He is not delaying it. It is simply that it takes longer for the timing of the event on the physical plane to coalesce with the event that has already happened on the higher level.

We are also responsible for when an event takes place. This is something people leave out of the equation altogether. We have a tremendous input into what happens and, therefore, the timing of any event. If we do nothing at all then it will happen at a certain time. But if we respond and act on our beliefs, we create circumstances that impose a time factor on that event – either to delay it longer or to bring it forward.

The people who are the most concerned and disappointed, the most longing for action on the part of Maitreya to make Himself known to the media, to get on with the work – these very people are the ones who do nothing at all to make it happen. They have never given a talk about Maitreya. They have never talked to anyone or told their family about what they really think and hope for. They keep it all to themselves like an inner secret.

We need to make things happen. "Man must act and implement his will," Maitreya says. "Nothing happens by itself." If we want something to happen we have to implement our will, and not just leave it to fate or Hierarchy or time or someone else to do it. We have to do it.

The 'star' that heralds Maitreya's emergence

On 12 December 2008 *Share International* distributed a news release announcing that in the very near future a large, bright star would appear in the sky, visible throughout the world, night and day, heralding the imminent appearance of Maitreya in His first interview on a major US television programme. Hundreds of sightings of the 'star' have since been recorded worldwide: videos of the 'star' have been posted on YouTube website creating much debate, television news programmes have reported sightings, and *Share International* magazine has received numerous photographs showing the 'star' in a variety of stunning colours and shapes. Included here is a small selection of photographs published in *Share International* and confirmed to be the 'star-like luminary'.

Boston, USA, 3 May 2010

Berlin, Germany, 3 March 2010

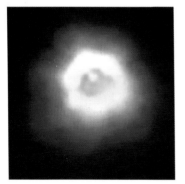

Oslo, Norway, 27 January 2009

Boston, USA, 11 April 2010

Permission by Dagfinn Rapp

Norwegian 'star' spiral

The enormous, spiral light with its glowing centre, seen over northern Norway on 9 December 2009 for almost 15 minutes, was reported by media worldwide and confirmed by Benjamin Creme's Master to be one of the four 'stars'.
photo: © Dagfinn Rapp

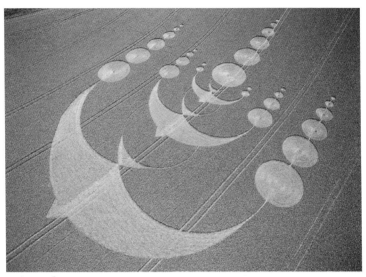

Crop formation - Adams Grave, Alton Barnes, Wiltshire - 4 August 2003

photo: © Steve Alexander

Crop formation - Hailey Wood, Ashbury, Oxon - 16 July 2007

photo: © Steve Alexander

Crop formation - Milk Hill, Wiltshire - 12 August 2001

photo: © Steve Alexander

www.temporarytemples.co.uk

THE 'HAND' OF MAITREYA

This photograph shows the handprint of Maitreya Himself, miraculously manifested on a bathroom mirror in Barcelona, Spain in 2001. It is not a simple handprint but a three-dimensional image with photographic detail.

By placing your hand over it, or simply looking at it, Maitreya's healing and help can be invoked (subject to Karmic Law). Until Maitreya emerges fully, and we see His face, it is the closest He can come to us.

"My help is yours to command, you have only to ask."
Maitreya, the World Teacher
from Message No. 49

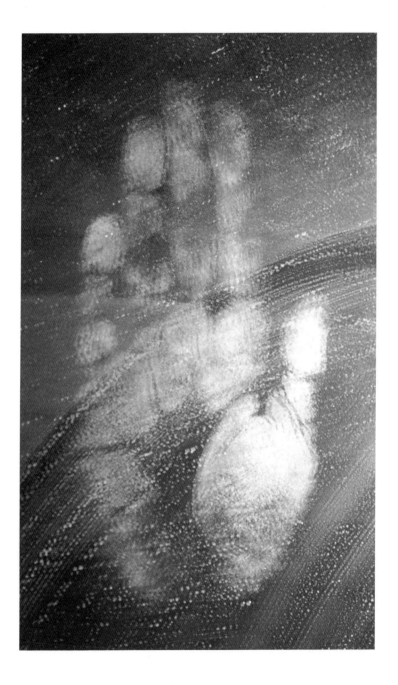

Jupiter UFO over Peru

This photograph, taken on 16 February 1989, in Valle Sagrado Urubamba, Peru, was confirmed by Benjamin Creme's Master to show a huge spaceship from the planet Jupiter. The craft, unseen by the people at the time, was in etheric matter, and was only visible when the film was developed.

PART TWO

EDUCATION IN THE NEW AGE

The three articles below by Benjamin Creme's Master are discussed by Benjamin Creme in his talk, 'New Age Education', and in the questions and answers which follow.

THE NEW EDUCATION
by the Master —, through Benjamin Creme

In seeking insights into the direction which education in the New Age might take, it will prove useful to establish the basic purpose which education serves and so throw light on the inadequacies of present educational approaches. Firstly, it must be understood for whom education exists and the process by which it carries out its function. This may be less obvious than at first sight may seem to be the case, for man has long been ignorant of his true nature and constitution, taking the part for the whole, and ignoring, to a large extent, his essential being.

Man, as a soul in incarnation, is an emerging God, and, through the Law of Rebirth, is advancing slowly to the demonstration, in full splendour, of that divinity. Education, in its true sense, is the means by which an individual, through a gradual expansion of conscious awareness, is fitted and fits himself for that goal. All that aids this process is education, however formal or informal the method might be.

In today's sense, education is a feeble thing indeed, ensuring only the minimum requirements for an understanding and control of man's environment. Few there are who learn more than the rudiments of life's meaning and purpose, caught up, as most people are, in the daily struggle for existence.

Whole nations, today, are all but illiterate still. Elsewhere, facts-full minds stand idle for lack of meaningful work. Education for jobs has replaced education for life while, more and more, the stresses and strains of such imbalance erupt in violence of all kinds.

Education should be understood as the means by which the indwelling God is contacted, known and given expression. Traditionally, religion has been seen to serve this purpose and religious education remains a bulwark in many countries today. However, religion is but one of many paths to God, and ways must be found which will allow all men to know and to express their experience of divinity.

To this end the new education should address itself. The fact of the soul, the Divine Intermediary, must gain general acceptance, and techniques of contact with this higher principle attain common usage.

When the ray structure, evolutionary development and purposes of the soul are known and documented, a more scientific approach can be made to the education of both children and adults, and a new meaning given to the process by which men learn to become Gods.

All of this awaits the earnest endeavours of those working in the educational field. Fitment for such tasks should be the aim of all aspiring to teach the young. Never has a better opportunity for service presented itself to those ready for the challenges of education for life in the New Age which now opens before us all. A new vista of possibilities will soon appear as men grapple with the problems of separation and division. This will release the forces and inspire the techniques of training and teaching which will bring men in due course to the feet of God.

(*Share International*, January 1988, and reprinted in *A Master Speaks*)

THE FAMILY

by the Master —, through Benjamin Creme

The family unit is the basis of all social life. Its importance cannot be over-emphasized. Today, this pre-eminence is being eroded by neglect, experiment and a misunderstanding of the essential needs of children.

All children need a stable background in which to grow and the exemplars of that process, a mother and father. That not all parents provide that stability or offer worthy examples is, sadly, all too true, and many factors are involved in this unfortunate condition: lack of education, poverty, inadequate housing, illness, and irresponsible and feckless adults, immature and unfit for the rigours of family life.

Let it also be said that millions in every country, poverty stricken and deprived of every amenity, strive valiantly, and mostly succeed against all the odds, to hold their families together and provide a stable and loving example to their young. They are the unsung heroes of the race who, through tenacity of purpose and endless self-sacrifice, represent the best that humanity can show.

The new education must address this fundamental problem and institute the training and requirements for family life. It is odd, is it not, that this most basic aspect of social life should receive such scant attention, and be left to the vagaries of chance to such a large extent?

In most countries, the right to drive a car is regulated and controlled by age and tests, more or less severe. Doctors and nurses, pilots and drivers of trains, all of them, may carry out their useful service only after due training and careful preparation. And rightly so. Yet millions of young people are allowed to enter this field of service – the most difficult in the world – for the most part devoid of training of any kind. The simple biological urge to reproduce, and the domination of the woman's 'time-clock', are considered sufficient to grant the right to multiply and add to a congested world.

The young couples commence the subtle and difficult art of upbringing and nourishing of souls in incarnation with little more than their conditioning to guide them. That conditioning they duly pass to their children and so the follies and ignorance perpetuate. Thus the need for the light of a new approach to this sacred service.

Today, there is an added and growing twist to the problem. Mounting sexual experimentation in the field of family life is leading to a distortion and misunderstanding of the true nature of the parent-child relation. The child is a soul in a family of souls. This provides the family unit with the opportunities for resolving karma developed over many incarnations together, in varying relationships.

Hierarchy is not the enemy of homosexuals, but the growing demand of homosexual men and women for the right to raise children is mistaken and unhelpful to the child.

All people, of whatever sexual persuasion, should think deeply about the nature and purpose of incarnation: the nurturing of souls who need a mother and a father to provide the examples, guidance and karmic opportunity to grow and evolve according to the Plan. If, for whatever reason, people feel inadequate to the task, a wise self-sacrifice for this life may be the wisest course.

(*Share International*, October 2002, and reprinted in *A Master Speaks*)

THE AGE OF LIGHT

by the Master —, through Benjamin Creme

In each century, a few men emerge who tower over their contemporaries. Their gifts are manifest, their genius shines forth for all to see and acclaim. We know them as the great discoverers, the painters, writers, musicians and scientists whose work has led humanity forward in a growing awareness of itself and its potential.

In recent times, their emphasis has been on science and the expansion of human knowledge. This has prepared the way for an extraordinary awakening of men's minds on a scale until now beyond hope of achievement. Man stands today on the threshold of a new enlightenment, of discoveries which will cast into the shade all previous accomplishments.

This coming time will be known as the Age of Light, and Light in all its meanings and manifestations will become the provenance of man. Already, the signs are there for the discerning that man is knocking on the door that leads to the Chamber of Light. Ancient darkness and ignorance are being banished as men grapple with the implications of new insights and technology. Soon, the Science of Light, the Divine Science, will be revealed to man's astonished gaze, and a major landmark on man's journey of evolution will have been reached.

Until now, only the specialist few have access to this Science of Light, but, already, steps are being taken to make its benefits available for all. The needs of all for power and light will be met safely and simply, the sun itself being harnessed in this cause.

United in love under the Banner of Maitreya, men will forge new pathways to the stars. As man explores her mysteries, nature will yield up her secrets, and reveal the ordered beauty underlying all.

Thus will begin a new and simpler life under the guidance of Maitreya and His Disciples. Cheerfully, men will relinquish the divisions of the past and enter into a new harmony with all that lives.

For long, men have searched in vain for the key to this yearned-for harmony. Always, their highest aspirations and efforts have been to no avail. Now, for the first time, the dawning realization of oneness is impressing men to share, and to regulate their living along more just and safer lines.

The new Era, the Era of Light, is upon us, and in this coming time men will find the inspiration and guidance which their forefathers lacked, or ignored. Now, at last, men and the Masters will work and move forward together, united in the common bond of Brotherhood and Trust. Our example will inspire men to superhuman efforts and achievements, and bring the Light into the hearts and minds of all. Thus will it be. Thus will the great secrets of creation be revealed. And thus will man become the creator and regulator of his own destiny, a God-like Being, worthy of the name of Man.

(*Share International*, September 1989, and reprinted in *A Master Speaks*)

NEW AGE EDUCATION

The following article is an edited version of a talk given by Benjamin Creme at the Transmission Meditation Conference held near San Francisco, USA, in August 2008. (Published in **Share International***, January/February 2009.) The quotations used are selected from the articles by Benjamin Creme's Master: 'The New Education', 'The Family', and 'The Age of Light', printed in the previous pages.*

The theme of this year's conference is 'New Age Education'. I am going to talk about a different type of education from that which exists today, with different aims, different ways and methods. If the direction is as suggested by the Master, it will entirely change education on planet Earth.

Basic purpose of education in the New Age

"In seeking insights into the directions which education in the New Age might take it will prove useful to establish the basic purpose which education serves and so throw light on the inadequacies of present educational approaches."

This is obviously true. If we do not know the purpose of education, if we do not know the nature of the being of the people we are being asked to educate, and if the present educational methods and approaches are not changed, then it is obvious we will not make much progress in training the young and adults for the experience of life in the new age.

Life in the new age will be completely different from all previous experiences on this planet. None of us, except the most evolved, will have gone through the stages of enlightenment, and the resulting growing meaningfulness of their lives, under the instruction of the Masters of Wisdom.

In this coming time the Masters will be living openly in the world. There are already 14 Masters plus Maitreya in the world. Eventually there will be about 40, though not all involved in education. However, a large number of the Masters are involved in education of some kind. Their disciples will become the teachers, in the first place, of the people who will most likely perform the main task of training and educating all groups, young and old, in this coming time.

As the nature of the human constitution and the aims of life on planet Earth are realized, as the world becomes more and more united through sharing, justice and peace, so more and more people will find in themselves the need to know: about who they are, their purpose in life, and their stage in evolution. People will talk a great deal about evolution, which will become the most significant factor on planet Earth. The evolution of human consciousness, and the development of all the kingdoms in nature, will dominate the thought and purpose of men and women everywhere.

As people become more aware of their identity as souls in incarnation, they will begin to express more of their soul quality. Therefore, the intuition will begin to work in people in whom it hardly plays a part today. More and more, we will intuit the possibilities and meanings behind the outer appearances of life.

We will want to know who we are in all aspects. Why were we born? Were we really born before? Are we really the result of a succession of lives through the Law of Rebirth?

Many people will take Maitreya's word for it on the Day of Declaration, but millions already believe in some way in reincarnation, especially Buddhists or Hindus. Millions of people will start asking questions. They will want to know how their age-long religious beliefs relate to the new information, the Ageless Wisdom Teachings given out by Hierarchy, which will be simplified in the beginning and then gradually approach the core of the truth.

People will begin to understand that humanity is travelling together as one huge group, at different stages of the evolutionary journey. We are all travelling together on a path to something tremendous which our minds at present find difficult to truly understand.

It is easy for a Master to say: "You become God-like beings who demonstrate all the qualities of God." We do not even know all the qualities of God. We think we know the intelligence of God. We have an inkling of what a mighty intelligence might be like, or a capacity to love totally and unconditionally and we imagine God's love must be like that. Something as mysterious as the Will of God will begin to attract the minds of many people. They will want to understand that extraordinary mystery – how the Will, the Purpose of God, can be known, what it is, how it demonstrates. What further aspects of God must we recognize in order to fully understand the aspects which we think we already know?

Over a period of time, all of this will begin to concern the minds of more people. If they are to make anything of it, they must be educated. It is that kind of education that the Master means when He talks about education for life, education for the new age, in which men and women recognize themselves as potential gods. If we recognize ourselves as a potential god, our aspiration grows accordingly. We want to become like that idea of divinity when the idea of being a soul really grips the imagination and rings true in the heart.

When you see Maitreya and the other Masters Who are coming out into the open with Him, you will see what God-like men look like, how They behave. What kind of inspiration must that be for humanity?

"Firstly, it must be understood for whom education exists and the process by which it carries out its function. This may be less obvious than at first sight may seem to be the case, for man has long been ignorant of his true nature and constitution, taking the part for the whole, and ignoring, to a large extent, his essential being."

According to the Masters, the human constitution is threefold. At the level with which we are familiar, it consists of the physical, the emotional and the mental bodies. One makes us want to eat, the other makes us feel sad or happy, as the case may be, and one tells us the time, that if we do not hurry we will miss the bus. For most people, this apparently solid physical body, which we see in the mirror, is all we are. You see yourself getting older as you look in the mirror, the jaw slacken, the lines grow under the eyes, the hair recede. Who or what is getting older? Only the body, which is only a vehicle. The true human constitution, according to the Masters, is that we are sparks of the divine. The divine is everywhere. In fact, there is nothing else but the divine. We live in a divine, spiritual universe. That is the nature of life.

We are the divine spark with all the potential of divinity. In this solar system, that potential will be at a certain level. In a higher solar system, like Sirius for example, we cannot yet know the nature of that divinity. It is infinitely creative, from our point of view always manifesting at ever-higher levels. On this planet, when we have brought that which is our highest into every aspect of that which is our lowest, we have completed the journey of evolution on planet Earth.

We are physical, we are the soul, we are the spark of God. That divine spark reflects itself as the individual human soul. The soul is an individualized part of one great Oversoul, which manifests as the human kingdom. The human soul is the intermediary between the divine spark (the Monad in Theosophical terminology) and the human personality on the physical plane. The three aspects – physical, emotional and mental – are the means by which the soul experiences life at the personality level.

If we see life clearly at this level on the physical, emotional and mental planes, the soul likewise experiences clearly. Unfortunately, so unevolved are the vast majority of people on planet Earth, that we do not present a sufficiently clear, pure view of life to allow the soul to see it adequately. The soul sees exactly what we present to it. It is a problem of illusion. Humanity lives in the illusion of its physical, emotional and mental view of life. On any of these three levels, if a person is seeing in an illusionary way that is the view of life they present to the soul.

The aim on the physical, emotional and mental planes is to purify the response to the world around us. We have done it more or less on the physical plane. I doubt if there are very many people today who are 'polarized', as it is called, on the physical plane. To be polarized on the physical plane means your thinking, your view of life, your seat of consciousness is the physical plane. Perhaps there are some people who are little more than intelligent animals.

Today 95 per cent of people are polarized on the astral plane, that is it is their seat of consciousness. This is a heavy weight on the evolution of humanity because the astral planes are specifically the planes of illusion. However, in this coming time this will begin to change. Already nearly 5 million people are standing at the threshold of the first of the five great planetary initiations that cover the last few lives of the evolutionary process on Earth and culminate in the resurrected, perfected Master.

The Plan of evolution is in the mind of that unbelievably high, evolved Cosmic Being Who ensouls planet Earth, our Planetary Logos. Our planet – with everything on it including ourselves and all the creatures that ever walked the Earth – is the means of expression of that great Being. He has a plan for the evolution of this planet in relation to the greater Plan of the Solar Logos. The Solar Logos is an even more advanced Cosmic Being, Whose body of expression is the solar system, including this and all the other planets. All planets have a Planetary Logos Whose plans relate to that of the Solar Logos. He has an even greater Plan because He sees a wider meaning and purpose beyond what the Planetary Logoi are seeing and working towards.

As far as planet Earth is concerned, the Custodians of this Plan are the Masters of Wisdom and the Lords of Compassion. Their task is to work out the Plan, through the human, subhuman and devic kingdoms insofar as this is possible. Not all the Masters will know all of the Plan, depending on Their status. The more advanced Masters like Maitreya will obviously know more of the purposes of the Logos than a Master of the fifth initiation, for example.

At each initiation, by token of the placing of the initiatory rod of power, the chakras of the initiate are heightened. The first two initiations are taken before Maitreya, and the third and higher ones before Sanat Kumara, the Lord of the World, on Shamballa. The initiations progressively give a greater and deeper sense of the extraordinary scope of the Plan.

The Plan touches on every aspect of life on planet Earth, and relates these different aspects to each other. Think of the human, animal, vegetable and mineral kingdoms, the extraordinary variety and scope of the devic, or angelic, evolutions: the subhuman elementals, the lower builders, the great devas whose bodies are so vast they could cover a continent. We cannot imagine the scope and variety of the devic evolutions. All these kingdoms and evolutions are interrelated. Nothing stands separate.

There is no separation in the whole of cosmos. Every atom is related to every other atom. This is behind the reality of the two great Laws that govern the evolutionary process. Some believe in them, some know them to be possible. To others they are facts. To some they are a nonsense, just fairy tales. The Law of Cause and Effect, the Law of Karma, and the associated Law of Rebirth govern the evolutionary process. Humanity as a whole has never been taught this. The information has been there for a long time, for anyone who wanted to avail themselves of it, but it is only the inquiring mind that has seized the opportunity. Only a very small number of humanity, especially in the West, take seriously the Law of Karma. They make jokes about it, but they do not actually believe it.

This Law relates everything to everything else. As you act, you set into motion a cause. As you speak, as you think, you likewise set into motion a cause. It is energetic.

We live in an energetic universe. There is only energy in the whole of cosmos, different energies vibrating at different rates. The rate of that vibration determines the form that the energy takes. It might be a galaxy, a solar system or a planet. It might be a rhinoceros or a human being. All of these are made of energy. There is nothing else but energy. This is the most basic tenet of esotericism. Modern science more and more has thrown light on this fact, but only the most interested and far out scientists have availed themselves of the knowledge. Everything that is matter can also be seen as energy. Everything that is energy likewise can be seen to precipitate downwards into matter. Matter and energy are part of one whole and interrelate as polarities of that one whole.

For centuries humanity has seen the physical body and says:

"That is me. That is Mr So-and-So and Mrs So-and-So over there. These are their children," and so on. That is true in a way but it is only part of the whole. The whole is a threefold Being: the divine spark, the soul and its vehicle, the personality, on the physical plane. The divine spark, unable to manifest at this level, creates its intermediary, the soul. The soul is a reflection of the divine, but vibrating at a slightly lower rate on its own plane in order to act as the intermediary between the highest and the lowest. What we take to be ourselves, this physical body, these emotions and this thinking mind, are only a vehicle, a means of allowing the soul to manifest through the dense physical.

In the process of evolution the physical body inevitably dies, and with it the emotional and mental bodies. They are part of the physical aspect of the threefold constitution. However, three permanent atoms remain, life after life: the dense-physical, the astral-emotional, and the mental permanent atoms. All the other atoms return to earth with the death of the physical body. These three permanent atoms are passed on from life to life, so ensuring the continuation of the genealogy of the person. What we were thousands of years ago is passed on to what we are now in this particular body, and will continue in successive bodies until we are a perfected Master. Around these three permanent atoms the soul creates the new body.

We are souls, absolutely and finally. If we think of ourselves as a soul, we think of ourselves in the right way. Unfortunately most people do not. If they are religious they probably believe in the soul, and think the soul is something they will meet when they die. True enough. You do meet your soul when you die, but you are your soul whether you are 'alive' or 'dead'.

Divinity, the highest aspect of ourselves, manifests through the soul at its level, and the soul manifests through its reflection, the personality, on the physical plane. The body of the child is set down in the womb by the soul, and brought to life by the soul to create another being through which it can demonstrate itself. If everything goes well, if we do not backslide, there is a succession of bodies, each one more perfectly demonstrating the qualities of the soul. The soul is who we are.

The Master Djwhal Khul, Who gave the Alice Bailey Teachings, wrote that one day the fact of the soul would be scientifically demonstrated. He said it could be that France would be given the honour of proving the fact of the soul.

We tend to take the part for the whole. Most scientists think that this physical body is all there is. We have a brain and that is what it is all about. It is a way of not seeing the forest for the trees. This is the result of the 5th Ray of Concrete Knowledge or Science, which is responsible for the tremendous expansion of human consciousness at the concrete level throughout the world. It expresses itself in our modern technology, which has made unbelievable strides in the last 100 years. Compared with the next 50 to 100 years even that will be as nothing, so great will be the transformation of life on Earth. So great will be the levels of understanding above the dense-physical that we will need a very different type of scientist who can get away from the blinkered view of seeing the part as the whole.

The influence of the 5th ray is both a boon and a hindrance. Over the last 150 years, the 5th ray has been in tremendous potency. A special effort has been made by Hierarchy to introduce this ray to humanity. It has opened up the human mind to all these extraordinary, intricate physical plane manifestations of communication. It has altered our view of the nature of technology. I am sure there are some minds that have leapt ahead of what is and see even more extraordinary developments.

The technicians of today tend, nevertheless, to see the part as being the whole, so a great opening for education awaits those who do know. I say "those who know", because much of what I am saying is not new to many of you. You know on some level that the part is not the whole and that there are other vistas, levels of Being, which must be given expression to fulfil the potential of man as gods.

You cannot present yourself as a god if you are not taught the means. All people are potential gods but they need education to fulfil that potential. All come into incarnation with the potential varying according to their level of evolution, but a potential altogether higher than they demonstrate today.

Whole nations, as the Master put it, are all but illiterate, even today. This is a terrible crime because literacy is easy and cheap. There is no nation in the world that should have a large percentage of its population illiterate. Yet there are millions of people, in many parts of the world, who are completely illiterate, who have to put a mark with their thumb when they sign their name. That is just a matter of education.

"Man, as a soul in incarnation, is an emerging God, and, through the Law of Rebirth, is advancing slowly to the demonstration, in full splendour, of that divinity. Education, in its true sense, is the means by which an individual, through a gradual expansion of conscious awareness, is fitted and fits himself for that goal. All that aids this process is education...."

This is the process by which the God in the heart of all people is given the possibility of manifesting. We need education to allow that to happen.

Education is a question of awareness. Through awareness we open ourselves to life, all things being equal allowing us to do so, as there are many social circumstances that hold back this process. Life is vibrating as energy, and by the growing conscious awareness of the meaning and effect of that energy, we evolve, we become more aware of the meaning and purpose of life.

It is an intuitive process. Our intuition is really conscious awareness. As it develops, as we become more and more like the nature of the soul, our consciousness becomes more like the soul. Through what we call intuition, which is a soul aspect, that consciousness becomes ours to demonstrate. You know because

119

you know. It is not the rational mind working it out. You have a rational mind for other rational purposes. If you want to catch a train, you go to a certain place at a certain time to catch that train. But if you want to understand, it is through the intuition that your awareness teaches you the nature of any particular experience.

As we go through the evolutionary process, through the five initiations which cover the last few lives of that process, the intuition grows because we grow as a soul. The divinity, the awareness and the light of the soul become manifest through the personality of the man or woman on the physical plane.

"All that aids this process is education, however formal or informal the method might be." When we think of education we usually think of going to school. You sit in lines taking tests. The teacher speaks and everyone sits back and listens. On the other hand, education can be totally informal. As the Master puts it: *"In today's sense, education is a feeble thing indeed, ensuring only the minimum requirements for an understanding and control of man's environment."*

It does not even do that. Look at what is happening to our global environment. We do not know what to do about it. It is beyond our understanding. It is beyond our ability to tackle. Unfortunately, some governments, like the present US government, do not even admit that it needs tackling, that there is anything wrong with our environment.

"Few there are who learn more than the rudiments of life's meaning and purpose ..." This is true because most people are in the daily struggle for existence. They have no time, energy or capacity to look for and find the necessary books or teacher to acquaint them with what they are looking for. People are looking for light, enlightenment, not simply how to get a better job.

"Whole nations, today, are all but illiterate still. Elsewhere, facts-full minds stand idle for lack of meaningful work."

Whole nations have filled their people's minds with facts, and that is considered education. They are not facts about the meaning and purpose of life. They are facts about how to work a computer, for example.

"Education for jobs has replaced education for life while, more and more, the stresses and strains of such imbalance erupt in violence of all kinds." People wonder why children are often so violent, why people do violent acts that have no seeming purpose. The terrible stress that people are living through in every country, the strain of life, the struggle just for existence, drains the sap out of people and leaves them withered and dry. Their view of life is dictated by the limits of commercialization. They see that if they do not have a university degree, they have no possibility of going beyond a menial job in most work fields today. That is destructive. People who feel like that can only see their own self-disgust and pain for so long without erupting in violence. "I am real!" they say. "I am real! I am as real as anybody else! I do not have money. I do not know how to get money because I have not had the education." This is the truth. People have not had education. They think the purpose of education is to get money. But the true goal of education is to understand who and what we are, what it is to be human, what is the purpose of life.

The most fundamental concept in life is that we are not separate. Most people feel separate. They feel alienated from society and from themselves as part of that society. So the violence escalates. They build themselves into little gangs. They do this as youngsters and then go into more sophisticated gangsterism. They get into drugs and wreck their lives and those around them. This causes a huge problem in their country.

It is a major problem in the United States. Drugs are involved in 90 per cent of all the crime in the USA. In England, it is about 85 per cent. It is much the same in France and Germany and every other so-called modern, educated country. We are not really educated because we are not educated for life. We are only educated for work. Some countries are better educated for work than others, so they do better in the competition that is the nature of commercialization and market forces. People compete in order to get the most, to be in front, to do better, to get the market. But that has nothing to do with real life.

"Education should be understood as the means by which the indwelling God is contacted, known and given expression."

How many carry out this purpose? Religion used to be thought to be the way: the priests knew better than everyone else and told everyone that God liked them or did not like them, depending on what they did. Humanity has to understand that all of us are gods. God is not to be found simply in the beliefs, dogmas and doctrines of any religion. There is no religion on Earth in which God exists. A religion can help you to understand and come into contact with what we call God; as Maitreya points out, religion is like a ladder, which can help you to get onto the roof. Once you are on the roof, you do not need the ladder.

"... religion is but one of many paths to God ..."

People have to know that God exists not only in religion, that you do not have to be religious to know God. God should demonstrate in every single human being, in every aspect of their life, every moment of every day. If all of us were in moment-to-moment contact with who and what we inwardly are, then that would happen. Every moment that divinity would shine through us, would decide what we do, would define what we are, how we behave, and how we understand and demonstrate that light which is divine. That is what we need education for.

"... ways must be found which will allow all men to know and to express their experience of divinity. To this end the new education should address itself. The fact of the soul, the Divine Intermediary, must gain general acceptance, and techniques of contact with this higher principle attain common usage."

Meditation of whatever kind will help you to come in contact with your soul; from Hierarchy's point of view Transmission Meditation is the most scientific.

Many people will take Maitreya's word for it after the Day of Declaration that we are souls, that we are divine. But how long will it last if the evidence of it is not forthcoming? It will take years of a colossal educational effort for the bulk of humanity to even have an intellectual understanding of the nature of the soul and of being a soul.

Once the principle of sharing is accepted and therefore the trust is created necessary for the ending of war, people will begin to find it easier to understand and accept inwardly, not just intellectually, the fact of the soul and "techniques of contact with this higher principle" will "attain common usage".

"All of this awaits the earnest endeavours of those working in the educational field." How many people in this room believe that they are equipped to work in the present-day educational field? There are a number of teachers here – this is your opportunity. *"Fitment for such tasks should be the aim of all aspiring to teach the young."* That is different from today. Fit yourselves for such tasks and you will fit yourselves for the new Age of Aquarius.

"Never has a better opportunity for service presented itself to those ready for the challenges of education for life in the New Age which now opens before us all. A new vista of possibilities will soon appear as men grapple with the problems of separation and division. This will release the forces and inspire the techniques of training and teaching which will bring men in due course to the feet of God."

As soon as we accept the principles of sharing, justice, right relationship, an end to war, freedom for all, these problems of separation and division will disappear. "This will release the forces and inspire the techniques of training and teaching" for life. That is the way forward for all.

123

The Age of Light

"In each century, a few men emerge who tower over their contemporaries. Their gifts are manifest, their genius shines forth for all to see and acclaim. We know them as the great discoverers, the painters, writers, musicians and scientists whose work has led humanity forward in a growing awareness of itself and its potential. In recent times, their emphasis has been on science and the expansion of human knowledge. This has prepared the way for an extraordinary awakening of men's minds on a scale until now beyond hope of achievement." There are many kinds of light. There is the light of knowledge. Knowledge itself is light. There is the light of the soul. There is the light of understanding, wisdom. There is physical plane light, the light from the sun, the light of electricity, which comes from the sun.

A new science, the Science of Light, will be instituted bit by bit as humanity becomes more aware of its oneness, and through sharing, justice and freedom for all, puts war far into the past as a means of action of any kind. When war is totally and utterly renounced, and the weapons of war destroyed, the Science of Light will be given to humanity. This is a tremendous science and already, as the Master says, steps are being taken that are making it practical.

We have created the worst possible weapon, the nuclear bomb. It is the most deadly weapon ever created by man and the most deadly weapon ever used by man. If used again it would lead to the destruction of all life on Earth, human and subhuman alike. So it must never be used. How can we get the nations to renounce war for ever, renounce the nuclear bomb, and also renounce their nuclear power stations, all that pertains to nuclear fission?

Humanity is well advanced on the wrong use of the energy of the atom. Nuclear fission is the most destructive use of energy that has ever been devised. Even today scientists and technicians are planning a vast increase of nuclear power stations all over the world to cope with global warming. The US is planning to build more than 50, France and Britain likewise, and generally around the world. If that were to happen, it would place an unbelievable extra burden on the health of humanity and the lower kingdoms.

Nuclear radiation above the level of gas is expelled into the atmosphere from every nuclear power station on Earth. This is also true of every stage of experiment with nuclear power involving bombs and various other weapons. This has increased tenfold the nuclear radiation extant in our atmosphere. But for the constant work of our Space Brothers – mainly from Mars and Venus, in their vehicles, the so-called UFOs – neutralizing the effect of this nuclear radiation, the health of humanity would be even more sorely stressed than it is today.

The Masters see pollution as the number one killer in the world. That includes nuclear radiation, which is the worst of all. The incidence of Alzheimer's disease has grown throughout the world, occurring at a younger and younger age. This is the direct result of nuclear radiation on the higher levels, which is pouring into our atmosphere every day and which we do not have the technology to measure.

Scientists must close the nuclear power stations as soon as possible and cease working on all manner of nuclear radiation now and into the future. This is a deadly mistake on the part of humanity, and is increasingly a threat to humanity's survival. Maitreya and the Masters in Their wisdom will communicate this information and recommend that the nuclear power plants be swiftly closed down.

Nuclear radiation and the other forms of pollution break down the human (and animal) immune system and leave us open to poisoning from the other toxic waste poured into our atmosphere. This problem must be swiftly dealt with before it becomes too great a burden even for the Space Brothers to overcome. They are allowed by karmic limits to deal only with a certain amount of our nuclear radiation and other pollution. Otherwise, it would be an infringement of our free will. They had to have special permission to do what they do. They spend long hours daily in every part of the world neutralizing and reducing the effect of nuclear radiation as well as the other noxious gases that we pour into our atmosphere. We owe the beings of those planets a huge karmic debt, which one day we will have to repay.

The Space Brothers are carrying out another tremendous operation. It is to do with the new Science of Light that is being brought into the world, ready for the day when we have renounced war and thus created peace and justice in the world. Without the renunciation of war there would never be the needed trust. No nation would trust the other nations not to have nuclear weapons hidden away.

The Technology of Light and crop circles

What is the connection between Mars, Venus, crop circles and the Technology of Light? The UFOs come mainly from Mars and Venus. The vast majority of them are made on Mars. They are made by thought and are guided by a combination of thought and technology. The Space Brothers also make the crop circles. These are essentially centres of force, vortices. The crop circles that have appeared all over the world are focused primarily in the south of England because that is where Maitreya is. His point of focus in the world is London. Although the crop circles are not in London, they are not far from there. They appear in large numbers in wheat and other crops for a reason. It is a tangential way for the beings in the spacecraft to leave their 'calling card', saying: "We were here."

The Space Brothers make incredibly intricate, beautiful, ever more elaborate patterns in the crop circles year after year. Then the crops are cut, the crop circles disappear, and they appear again the next year when they are made again. They are deliberately put in crops because the crops are seasonal. Similar 'crop circles' are made all over the world. They are on mountains, in oceans, in the seas, in the rivers, on the land. The crops only give them visual patterns. They appear in crop circles so that we know that they occur, but they are manifested everywhere. Some of the patterns, especially the more recent ones, have meaning. As soon as they are seen, people say, for example: "That stands for Pi in geometry."

Around this planet, as around all planets, is a magnetic field. It is made up of lines of force that criss-cross each other. Where they intersect a number of times, they form a vortex. It is like a chakra, a vortex of power. The Space Brothers are creating these vortices of power on the physical plane. A crop circle is really an outer sign of a vortex. A replica of our planet's magnetic field is being placed all over the physical world, not as huge and powerful as the planet's magnetic field, but powerful and widespread enough to be the basis of the Technology of Light.

The light will come directly from the sun and be fused with the magnetism of the magnetic field. That will give humanity every form of power it needs. All our mechanical objects, our heat, our light, our transport, our cooking, our machinery will be powered by this Technology of Light, using light from the sun and the magnetism of our planet's magnetic field. There will be large storehouses made in specific shapes. The shapes themselves will be related to the type of energy they store. From these storehouses will come this unlimited power for all our needs.

Trains, for example, will seem to be motionless. We will be sitting in them talking and not even notice that we are moving. They will be very fast and utterly still and silent. Travel fatigue will disappear. We will go on a long train ride and when we finish our journey, it will be as if we had not moved. We will be just as relaxed as when we started.

This power will satisfy all our energy needs. It will power spaceships that will take people across the galaxy. In your next life, you might be a discoverer of planets and solar systems out there that are peopled by … we do not know. They will be men, of course, although they might not look exactly like us. But they are men nevertheless. Man is everywhere in cosmos. You will be able to go as far as you like out into space and it will not take any time. Time really does not exist.

Energies of Aquarius

Humanity will come into the total understanding that we are one group called humanity, that there is nothing separate in the whole of cosmos, that everything relates to everything else, that the laws that connect humanity are the laws built out of the non-existence of cleavage of any kind throughout cosmos. We will grow with the impact of the energies of synthesis, streaming to us from Aquarius, into this sense of being fused and blended together. That is the essence of the energies of Aquarius. They only work through the group. The energies do not work through individuals. Individuality will not disappear, but will be placed at the service of the group.

People today are only too willing to demonstrate their individuality. That is why they can be so destructive, because that individuality is often in the hands of people in positions of power but who are not evolved enough to handle that power. They invade other countries, wage war and make life hell for millions of people. That so-cherished individuality of which we are rightly proud must be put at the service of the group.

Aquarius is about the group. It is about bringing unity, synthesis into the greatest number of individual parts. It is not to obliterate individuality. It is not to get rid of the parts, the differences. On the contrary, it is to synthesize into a total unity the greatest number of different individual parts. It is unity in diversity. That should be the slogan for all future work.

Unity with the maximum diversity is the aim of all those ready and willing to work in line with the new Age of Aquarius.

As individuals grow, as they become more and more imbued with the energy and light of their soul, they will want to serve because that is what the soul wants to do. The soul's purpose is to serve the Plan of evolution in the mind of the Logos. That is why the soul comes into incarnation in the first place, and in so doing brings the Plan to fruition.

In this time, under the influence, inspiration and example of the Masters, as people want more and more to serve, the soul will make it possible. No one will be left without a field of service. The Masters are here to serve the Plan and to inspire humanity to carry out their soul's purpose.

(*Share International*, January/February 2009)

WE DO NOT KNOW WHO WE ARE

Why did you pair those two articles together, 'The New Education' and 'The Age of Light'? (March 2009)
They are part of a threesome. 'The New Education', 'The Age of Light' and 'The Family' are related in important ways: 'The New Education', on education in the outer world, schools, business, in all situations; 'The Age of Light' about the new approach to education which that age will bring; and 'The Family' – in the most immediate sense how the education of children and the family can best be done. I thought those three articles gave three aspects of education, each closely related to the other. The Master has written so many articles, often about the same subjects in different ways. I could have probably taken three other articles and used those to do the same thing.

What does Maitreya mean by "honesty of mind", "sincerity of spirit" and "detachment"? (March 2009)
We have a threefold constitution. We are the monad, the divine spark, reflecting as the divine soul on its own level. We are also the ensouled personality, however unaware we might be.

Everything works out in threes. When we are at our highest, we reflect the spark of God, the divine, the spiritual. When we are nearly at our highest, we reflect the soul. It is the intermediary. If you are in right relation to the soul, you are in right relation to that of which the soul is a reflection.

On the physical personality level there may be a degree of contact with the soul, but none with the highest aspect, the monad, except through the soul, the intermediary. It acts as an intermediary for as long as it takes to bring its reflection, the human personality, into right relationship with the monad.

Since we have a physical, an astral and a mental body, everything necessarily reflects through these three. Honesty of mind is obviously to do with the mind. Most people do not have honesty of mind. If we thought about our habitual use of the mind, we would find that as often as not we think one thing, say something else, and do something else again. There is no direct line from the thought to the deed.

Sincerity of spirit relates to the sensitive, astral feeling body. Maitreya says the best way to think about this is to think of talking to some well-loved person, an associate or old friend whom you trust. You speak with that person honestly. You do not expect him or her to be indulgent of you. You do not try to put anything over on such a person, or try to get them to have a better view of you. You trust them to be open to you, to speak to you as you believe, think and feel yourself to be, heart-to-heart. Only two old friends can have a heart-to-heart talk, where they trust each other and accept the other as they are. Sincerity of spirit is obviously related to honesty of mind. They are not so very different.

Detachment is the highest level, the detachment of the soul. The soul is detached. It does not want or need anything. It has only the desire to serve the Plan. The soul tries to influence and bring its reflection, the man or woman, into the position of serving the Plan. That takes what we would call a long time.

From the soul's point of view, there is no time. It is an endless vista of eternity, so the soul is not in a hurry. But it tries constantly, life after life, to impress its vehicle to develop a growing detachment – from seeing oneself as the physical body; from dishonesty, therefore, of mind; from insincerity of spirit, from the glamour of needing to be loved, needing to be treated gently and indulged.

If people are really detached, insincerity does not affect them. It can be a nuisance, but that kind of insincerity is simply the agitation in the core of the person. They are not detached in themselves. They want you to love them. People are always hungry for love. They want to belong. They want to be made to feel good. They want to be inspired. They want all these things.

Fundamentally, if you are working at the soul level at all, you become more and more detached. That detachment is the highest; it is the aim. As you become more detached, you become more honest in mind, more sincere in spirit. As you become more honest in mind and more sincere in spirit, you become more detached. These three things work together.

These are the three key things presented by Maitreya as the base of His teachings. If we only practised them to any real extent, we would achieve much.

You said we can either have the experience of oneness or separateness but not both at the same time. What suggestion can you offer on how to live in oneness more often than not, day in, day out? (March 2009)

It is an inner sense of belonging to the group we call humanity. We are not only a group of people, we, humanity, are an energetic centre in the world. There are three such centres: the human kingdom, the centre where the Intelligence of God manifests; Hierarchy, the centre where the Love of God is expressed; and Shamballa, the centre where the Will and Purpose of God is known. These are the three great centres of energy on planet Earth. The human kingdom is to do with knowing, the growth of mind. We are in the process of perfecting the mind aspect of man.

The physical body of man is more or less perfected. There will be very slight changes, growing awarenesses, especially in the eyes so that the etheric levels will become visible to sight as more and more children who have etheric vision come into incarnation. They will become so many that the etheric will be recognized as real.

Perfecting the intelligence or mind aspect of divinity is a huge responsibility. We will develop our minds until we can create by thought, for example, this magnifying glass, these spectacles, this table. This may seem impossible now but it is already a reality, for example, on Mars. The Martians make most of the spacecraft which we call UFOs, by thought, some of which are miles long. Can you imagine a spaceship four or five miles long, just outside our atmosphere, floating out there in space, filled with laboratories of all kinds and spaceships? They open a hangar and let the spaceships out, one after another. It is a huge town-like edifice, but it is a spaceship made by thought.

Can you imagine creating a table by thought? Humanity will develop its mind to the extent of creating by thought all the artefacts of our modern civilization. Not at first, not for some time, but in the not too distant future men's minds will be expanded to an extent that we will have a different notion of what it is to think.

Will you explain more about "a different notion of what it is to think"? (March 2009)
Thinking is the ability to create by thought. When you create a painting, you are creating by thought. Your thought goes into it. It does not happen by itself. You have to have the idea. You have to have the hand and eye co-ordination to bring the idea onto the physical plane surface of the canvas or whatever is your

medium. If your medium is music, you have to create by thought all the sequences that make a piece of music.

Mozart did that, but he did not see it as you might think, as music written out that he was able to write down. He did not see the notes with his inner eye and copy them down. He saw the music like a flat painting. But he understood it not as a painting but as music. He copied down in musical terms what he saw as a painted object. By looking at that, he knew what the music should be. That is the creative mind.

It depends on your receptivity, how your mind works. Someone with a visual sense would paint a picture. Someone with a musical sense would write music. For both of them it is the same activity; the creative mind is doing it. By mind, I do not mean the brain. The mind is different from the brain.

Scientists are still discussing whether we have a mind at all or just a brain. They know we have a brain because they can look at it. They can conduct experiments and perform operations on the brain. But they cannot perform an operation on the mind because the mind is other than the brain, although it is related to the brain by contact, as in a computer.

The mind is an energy belt that permeates all space into which the ideas or formulae of the Masters are placed. When these are ripe for use, they are tuned into by the sensitive minds of the race. Scientists such as Einstein discover great scientific theories. Practical, technical scientists discover how to develop the computer, for example. All of that is put there in the mind belt. It takes the sensitive minds of the discoverers, scientists, painters or musicians to bring the ideas down and make them useable.

When we have developed our minds more, we will discover how to create factories and, in the factories, tools like robots that will create all the things we need from our thought. It is extraordinary to think of, but if it is not just around the corner, it is around the corner after that.

Famed Canadian neuroscientist Wilder Penfield thought that the mind may interface with the brain in part of the diencephalon. (1) Is that true? (2) If so, is there a specific part of the diencephalon that you can identify where the mind interfaces with the brain? (November 2008)

(1) Yes. (2) It is not in a part of, but in the diencephalon.

(1) What is the difference between how memory is stored in the mind versus the brain? I am sure that the mind stores memory, but does the brain also store memory? (2) There is a limit to how much memory can be stored in the brain, but not in the mind, correct? (3) Can you explain the relationship of the mind and the brain? (May 2009)

(1) The brain stores memory and makes it generally available. The mind does not 'store' memory but has access to it if developed enough. (2) One cannot generalize. Theoretically, there is no limit to what the brain can store, but it depends on the development and health of the person. Likewise, the access of the mind to memory is only limited by development and awareness. (3) The brain is an instrument, highly developed and capable of further development but part of our physical apparatus. The mind has access, in a healthy person, to the stored memory of the brain.

It is said only 10 per cent of the brain is used. What percentage is used by high initiates and how much is used by other people? Is it really only 10 per cent? (January/February 2009)

The average person uses about 12 per cent of his possible brain functions. An initiate of say the third degree would probably be using 60 to 70 per cent of his brain function.

The latest research seems to suggest that during puberty there is a new development, even growth, of the brain. The same research appears to indicate that if the brain is creatively, actively, usefully used and 'exercised' at this time it creates a

134

long-lasting positive enhancement of brain capacity. Is there any truth in this? (September 2002)

Yes. It is 100 per cent true.

At the beginning of your lectures you ask the audience to keep an open mind. What does an open mind really mean? How can we be open-minded? (September 2002)

To be open-minded doesn't mean to be empty-minded. It means not to be prejudiced. To every new idea we bring to it what is really our conditioning, our prejudices built from the cradle onwards, by our parents, teachers, the life we lead, the things we read and so on. That creates thoughtforms in our mind which then become fixed and they prevent us from seeing something else. Being open-minded means being free. It means having a mind which belongs to yourself with nothing in it which prevents you from looking objectively at new information.

Most people, when they hear new information, bring up their preconception of what that is. If they like it they accept it. If they don't like it they tend to reject it. But on the level of mind there is neither liking nor disliking. There is only what is true. If it is true it is interesting. It may not be your path but it is interesting. It has the ring of truth because you have not put something else in its place and rejected it. If you are free in this sense your mind is open and you begin to learn, to self-educate. You can test in yourself whether it is true or not. If it is true you can see it in connection with everything else. If it is false it doesn't fit in with anything else. You can immediately test it and see that it is false. The truth has its own power, the power of being which nothing can destroy.

How can one open the mind more – become less rigid or set in one's beliefs? (November 2008)

Become more tolerant of difference. Meet more people of opposing views and try to understand their point of view.

What is the difference between true and false hope? (November 2009)

True hope emanates from the soul and is therefore a spiritual quality. It fills the person with the desire to seek and visualize an aspiration for future betterment and is therefore a driving force for evolution itself. That is why, for humanity, hope is an essential aspect of life.

False hope, on the other hand, is the expression of an emotional desire for belief, help and security. It is essentially the outcome of fear and frequently leads to disappointment.

There seems to be a consensus among developmental psychologists today that a person's identity is the product of the cultural and family background, the school environment, and the peer group. Since this leaves out the notion of the soul reincarnating for its own purpose, could you elaborate on the role of the soul in the formation of our identity? (July/August 2005)

A person's personality is – to some extent – the product of the various influences mentioned in the question. But the personality is not the identity. Each of us is a soul in incarnation and, more and more, shows itself as the identity through the personality. The trouble is that – for the most part – developmental psychologists reject the notion of the soul. Psychology will make no further progress until it recognizes the fact of the soul.

Sigmund Freud's theory about how the personality is formed has had a huge impact on Western thought about human development, even if many psychologists now dispute most of his theories and claims. Is any of his work still relevant or useful from the Masters' point of view? (July/August 2005)

Yes. For example he has thrown light on the reality of the unconscious mind and its effects on the actions of most people.

*In the introduction to her book **The Soul and its Mechanism**, Alice Bailey says that Western psychology, with its emphasis on behaviourism (man is the product of his environment; the 'materialistic' view of man), needs to be complemented with the introspective psychology of the East, based on the precept of an inner driving force, the soul, for a more comprehensive and realistic view. Does it follow that there is a role for behaviourism in raising and educating children, in conjunction with the constructivist approach to human learning and development?* (July/August 2005)

Yes, the environment has, obviously, an influence on the development of the personality but even so it is only around 30 per cent where the average person is concerned. It becomes considerably less influential in the case of the advancing initiate who is demonstrating more of his/her soul quality.

INTUITION AND CREATIVITY

I understand that one should try to develop one's intuition. (1) How do you do that? (2) Is it the same as just thinking through a problem rationally and clearly? (3) What would hinder the development of intuition? (May 2001)

(1) Intuition comes from the soul. Therefore, whatever invokes the soul develops intuition. Meditation and service are the age-old royal ways to the soul. It is advisable to read the Alice Bailey books (Lucis Press). They are written by the Master Djwhal Khul in such a way as to awaken the intuition. (2) No. It is seeing it from the point of view of the soul. (3) Some rays (2,4,6) are more conducive to the development of intuition because they give quicker, easier access to the soul.

Reading the Yoga Sutras of Patanjali I came across the idea of 'spiritual reading'; I gather this means the understanding and

137

pondering of symbols. Could you explain what advantage there is to reflecting on the symbolic nature of things? (July/August 2001)

It is necessary in the training of the abstract mind.

How can the use of the intuition help us educate? How can education help develop the intuition? How does this relate to the education of people as souls? (March 2009)

Without the faculty of intuition, which is a soul aspect, I do not know that you can educate anyone at all. If you do not have intuition, you cannot sense the need of the person you are educating. Those who educate people from 14 to 18 years of age, for example, need to be able to sense where they are in evolution. You do not have to necessarily say they are 1.358 or 0.72. It need not be as precise as that. But you know that they are coming up towards the first initiation, or have probably taken the first initiation, but are not much beyond that. By what they present to you, they might be around 1.5 or 1.6 and making the shift from astral to mental polarization. You can sense this by the use of the intuition. That intuition is based on practical knowledge, experience; that is number one. But intuition is primarily a soul function and if you are functioning as a soul, you know because you know; you are not using ratiocination.

However, I have met many people who think they know because they know – but they are wrong! What they take to be intuition is not intuition at all. It is simply their glamour. There is a glamour that they mistake for intuition, as there is a glamour they mistake for knowledge. You have to be able to differentiate between glamour and intuition.

Intuition is a faculty of the soul, which knows everything on its own plane. The soul knows the past, present and future. It is not involved in time. One aspect of that which we call intuition develops as you raise your consciousness closer to the vibration of the soul.

How do you paint a picture? You do it by intuition.

What makes a painter know what to paint or a musician know what notes to write? Something is guiding him. Mozart, Beethoven, Rembrandt, Leonardo are doing it by intuition. You have a canvas and there is nothing on it. There are sheets of paper with lines on them but no notes. How does that become the manuscript of music, a symphony, for example? How does a canvas become a painting? A canvas is only a support for a painting. How do you get the painting? How does a painter know what to put there? With colour you can put red, yellow, blue, green, violet. You can go through the gamut of them all, but most painters do not. Some do and you see the result. Something makes you choose. What is it that makes you choose? You choose a red and a blue, or a yellow and a violet. You choose them at a certain hue of that colour and a certain tone of that hue. All the time you are relating the hue and tone of one colour to the hue and tone of another colour. They might be side by side or across the painting. All that is related to intuition. You do it because you know what to do, but you do not know what to do until you start doing it.

How can the use of the intuition help us to educate? The intuition is necessary; otherwise you cannot educate. You may be trained as a teacher, go to college and have your brain filled with facts. You apply those facts and that is educating children. But for what? Certainly not for life. It is educating children for the thoughtform in the minds of the country's professional educators. The facts imparted by these trained teachers will fit these students for such-and-such a level of work. It does not in any real sense draw on the faculty of the intuition. That is not to say that some teachers will not have intuition and I am sure many do.

You cannot be a painter, a musician, a scientist or a teacher at any level at all without the use of the intuition. It is the intuition that tells you that such and such is so. How did Einstein get to $E=mc^2$? That is intuition. Einstein could not do simple arithmetic, but he could find the most fantastic formula that relates energy to matter. Energy equals mass times the speed of light squared. It is an extraordinary awareness, which you can only arrive at by intuition. The great discoverers use intuition, and that comes from the soul. Einstein was a second-degree initiate, obviously in touch with the soul and receptive to the soul's impress. He did not set out to educate the world, but the world has been educated dramatically by his formula, his understanding. He was educating the people of his time.

How does this relate to the education of people as souls? To bring the soul more and more into the life of the person, we have two processes – meditation and service. Nothing helps us to invoke the soul more than meditation and service. They are the given tools, the path for becoming soul infused. Soul infusion is very slow, it develops bit by bit. Yet every life takes the person closer to the soul. There might be some very lazy lives or backward-sliding lives when nothing much is taken in. But if all goes well the soul imparts its light to the person. Each individual's atomic particles are gradually changed to subatomic particles. Instead of atomic particles, the body is made up of more and more of these light particles, more of the nature of the soul.

As the person meditates and serves in the correct way, altruistically, without sense of self, they automatically absorb light from the soul, which in their meditation they are invoking all the time. The soul gives of its light to the developing person, and the bodies change. By the end of the journey the person is totally subatomic or light. He is a Master. One major difference in a sense between a Master and ourselves is that if you could see, visually, the body of a Master, you would see that it is totally light, while ours is atomic with a degree of subatomic particles of light.

The soul is all light; it is energy. It does not need a physical body. The Masters per se do not need a physical body. Many of

Them have a physical body, but many of Them work in Their etheric body. A physical body is only needed when the light is needed to be seen. Normally what we call light manifests without a physical body. The higher the light, the less is the need for a physical apparatus. We are light, but we need a physical body for us to see the light. When we turn on the electricity, we see the light that comes on as a result. But that electricity itself does not need an electrical set up to demonstrate. We need it, but the electricity, which is a physical-plane level of electrical fire in the sun, has no physical body. The Central Spiritual Sun, which is light itself, manifests at this physical plane level as electrical light or heat.

The ensouling process goes on as we meditate and serve. Once you are ensouled, even a little, you cannot be anything else but ensouled.

What are the characteristics of a soul-infused person? How do we manifest soul infusion? (March 2009)
We do not. That is the trouble. What is a soul-infused person? Think of someone at the very best you can imagine: wise, kind, full of knowledge and light and respect for all, filled with enthusiasm for life, justice and sharing. Those are the characteristics of a somewhat soul-infused person.

What is the importance of creativity for education? (January/February 2009)
It is what education is about; it is what life is about. Education is about fitting humanity for the creative awareness of its purpose in life and of the means by which this may be fulfilled. It is about preparing a being, an immortal god. We have to accept that we are immortal gods, deathless gods at the full level of divinity of this planet. This planet is not the highest in the system and not in a very high system. It is a relative thing, but within that relativity these potential gods are looking to the educators for the ways and means of living to allow that divinity to

manifest. That is all that is lacking: to bring out to the full every part of the potential which in any particular life is theirs to give.

Because of the Law of Rebirth we have to treat it life by life. That makes it possible. There is no way you can give to the person at the beginning of the evolutionary journey all that she/he will need to become a god because the apparatus is not yet developed: the brain is not evolved enough, the physical body is not strong enough, the astral body is not quiet enough, the mental body is not sufficiently filled with the necessary knowledge to be taught.

Teaching is about giving to an open but as yet limited mind the precepts, the understandings, the knowledge of what it is to be human and how to live with other humans in peace, with justice and freedom for all. It is a colossal task, not easy by any means. But it is a creative task.

The essence of all art, all science, all philosophy, all religion is creativity. We live in a spiritual universe. That spiritual universe is a constantly changing motor, a kind of great generator of creativity that generates different aspects of that creativity and throws them out into the universe, when they trickle down through the various galaxies and solar systems. These energies of creativity come to little planet Earth as distant echoes of an idea. That idea can galvanize and transform the world. It is as strange, as simple and as gigantic as that.

These great ideas are pouring into our space. But they take time to come down and our minds have to be attuned like a growing conscious awareness to their meaning and their effect on our lives, and we have to find the best way to put them into effect. That is the nature of life.

We are souls in incarnation and therefore creative. That is the nature of our life. You cannot say: "Well, a bit of it will be creative, but another bit does not need to be." Everything has to be creative moment to moment. Creativity is not something you can put on like butter on bread, just to make it tastier. Creativity is the very stuff, the nature, of life. When life is sensed correctly it is seen as meaningful, purposeful, and when we grasp the meaning and purpose of life it leads to that creativity being born in us, however we give it expression. We give it expression, of course, as a man or woman according to our previous lives' experience.

We have to live in that creative state as part of our everyday being. So it is not something we do when we have time. It is something we do because it is something we are. If we are creative then we are always creative. Even if we do not seem to be doing anything we can still be creative. Creativity is a state of being, of being-ness. The closer we maintain our focus and concentrated awareness in our everyday life, the closer we are to that creative state. And that is Divinity. It is creation. It is what life is. It is what we are, what everyone is.

Can you comment on the value of personal experience in the role of education – for example, the Day of Declaration? (March 2009)
Nothing is as valuable as personal experience of whatever kind. The personal experience of the Day of Declaration will be extraordinarily transforming. For a few weeks perhaps people will feel and behave differently. They will like each other. They will say "hello" in the street. You know from experience better in every way than anything you hear from someone else. No one can take that away from you. I know the Christ is in the world because I have experienced it. When I talk about it, I present it for consideration, but I know it. That is why I can talk about it with conviction. Anything that is the result of experience will be altogether more transforming than something you hear about from someone else.

Will most people feel their own soul on the Day of Declaration when Maitreya is speaking? (April 2009)

143

Most people will experience their own souls, even if it is the first time in their lives. It will be an extraordinary experience for humanity. They will feel like a child: pure, listening from the heart to these wonderful words and experiencing a quality of life that they have forgotten – that goes way back to their childhood when they were simple, trusting, full of love and happiness.

Will it make a difference in our next incarnation if we have the experience of the Day of Declaration in this life? (March 2009) How could it not? If the Day of Declaration is even remotely like what I understand it to be, we will be changed as never before in our lives. All of us, everyone on Earth, will be changed to some degree. Perhaps the absolute hard-edged fundamentalists of whatever religion will not be all that happy to have received the experience, and will perhaps not attach any great importance to it, but it will have changed them. No one can go through what they will experience on the Day of Declaration and not be changed in some way.

The changes in our sense of being will be profound, and the emotions arising from that will last for weeks. The Master said: "Humanity will walk on tiptoe for a time."

Then reality will set in again. The problems will still be there. We will still have the pain and suffering of millions starving to death. We will still have the environment to cope with – how to rid the world of global warming and stop the destruction of the planet. The world's problems will take form again in the minds of millions.

But millions will be recharged in their sense of themselves as being human, and feel that they count for the first time in their lives. They will have gone through an extraordinary spiritual experience, which will cleanse them. The Master said: *"Each ... will experience anew the grace of childhood, the purity of aspiration cleansed of self."* People will be like children again. We will see the world as children do, with a sense of grace, joy, wonder and simple acceptance, taking everything on trust. The sense of trust will grow in humanity for the first time in thousands of years.

Today no one trusts life sufficiently. Everyone is hardened and feels they have to harden themselves because of commercialization, striving for a living in a place where only the market counts. At the heart of life there is competition.

Co-operation is the nature of life for humanity. When man finds his true interior being as a soul, competition drops away of its own accord and, with it, the lie of commercialization. Every person, without exception, is divine.

*In her last book **From the Mundane to the Magnificent** (1979), esotericist Vera Stanley Alder describes an intriguing episode in her life, which took place in 1942. She relates how an advanced being, whom she calls Raphael, takes it upon himself to reveal to her aspects of reality in a series of 'hands-on' experiences on the inner planes. In the last of these lessons he grants her wish for a vision of the future. When asked how such a brilliant future could ever be realized, Raphael assures her that this will be possible through the intervention in the near future of the "Coming One", the Christ, known in the east as Maitreya Buddha.*

(1) Can you say whether this experience took place in 1942, three years before Maitreya's decision to return at the earliest possible moment? (2) Was Raphael merely settling a karmic debt, as he told Mrs Alder, or did/does he have a specific part to play as regards Maitreya's return? (3) Do you know if Mrs Alder ever received confirmation of her experience by way of your information, before she died in 1984? (September 2001)

(1) Yes. Outside the physical brain, time does not exist. (2) Both. (3) Yes. She contacted me and we met at her home in Bournemouth, England.

How receptive, from the Hierarchy's point of view, is humanity at present to Maitreya's ideas? Does increased fear and tension close people psychologically to His priorities? (December 2002)
No, the opposite. Fear drives people to act hysterically – as in the US today – or to look for answers to the problems.

Why do people fear difference – different cultures, religions and so on? What is so frightening about 'otherness'? (June 2004)
Because it is unknown and, therefore, possibly dangerous.

The Master's article 'The missing link' (January/February 2002) mentioned that humanity had completed its apprenticeship. Looking around, one could be forgiven for thinking we have learned nothing! What does the Master mean? (March 2002)
That humanity has 'come of age', become adult. From the esoteric point of view this is the case. For the first time in our long history, the personality vehicles (mental, astral, physical) are now occultly integrated and aligned correctly to the soul on a world scale. That is not to say, of course, that, from a vibrational point of view, the rate of each vehicle is synchronous.

EDUCATING YOUNG CHILDREN

How can we avoid conditioning a child and how do we respect his or her free will yet provide stability and safety by healthy regulation? (January/February 2009)
That is the 64 billion-dollar question. In the world as it is at the moment, it is almost impossible to do that. That does not mean that we should not try.

We have to watch ourselves. We have to be very aware of ourselves and of the child's reactions. Let the child regulate him or herself. Praising a child for something they have done well strengthens their self-confidence but constant over-praise can distort their sense of self in relation to others. On the other hand,

146

condemnation and punishment of any kind should never be resorted to.

The child is only a child and is just being the little animal it really is at this stage. It acts completely from instinct and needs to be loved, petted, nurtured and amused, and listened to and carefully tuned to the possibilities of life. So when it is asked to be quiet, it can learn to be quiet. When it is asked to not do certain things, it can learn without punishment to not do certain things. This takes patience. The parent has to be patient and never expect the child to be patient because the child does not know what it is to be patient.

But children are wise, even young children are very wise and aware of the mother and father, and family and people around them. They become very aware of other people as personalities and notice very directly, and yet subtly, what they are experiencing – love or hate, dislike or impatience, or whatever.

It takes great sensitivity not to harm the child, not to infringe its free will and avoid imposing your solution on whatever is the problem. Bringing up a child is always an act of compromise.

In this less than perfect world today people inevitably are less than perfect and should not expect too much from themselves or harm themselves by too strong self-criticism. And they should not in any way harm the child by criticism. The child does not know because it does not see life in the way that older people do. People sometimes treat children as if they were an adult or older person. But the child is not yet a fully conscious human being. Its consciousness is limited. If they are very young, they may still be living in their previous incarnational experience.

So there is no simple answer to this question. First and foremost you have to like the child. And, unfortunately, a lot of parents love the child, but at times they may not like it because they have an unspoken resentment of it for infringing their freedom. The child is always there – demanding and demanding

– and perhaps the parents have little money. They cannot fulfil the child's demands and blame the child, and harm the child unconsciously, without meaning to. I have seen this done forcefully and powerfully by hitting and screaming and swearing at the child. But this often comes from ignorance and exhaustion. We hand on our conditioning.

You ask how can you avoid conditioning the child. Well, if you are an ordinary human being, you cannot. We are not perfect. We will not be perfect until the world is more perfect.

We can try to be better and that is the most we can do. Remember to love the child under all conditions, in whatever situation, even when they are driving you mad. It is difficult, but that is life.

Outside of practising a religion and our meditation, please give a few examples of how parents can educate their children to know, contact and give expression to the indwelling God. (March 2009)

The best way is by example. You do not talk to your children about God. Young children do not know anything about God. They should be left to find God within themselves and to express their sense of it for themselves. We should not give them a thoughtform of God, nor give them meditations to bring the soul into manifestation. We should teach by example. Children are sponges. They mop up what we present to them. We present ourselves to them as all-knowing, all-suffering, patient, loving (in every way a doormat!), then they accept it and will demonstrate their soul qualities.

We have to be willing to completely devote ourselves to the child or children. How many people can do that? We usually have jobs to do, and are busy and frightened ourselves. We cannot help but pass on that fear and sense of rush. No one has any time. We are dominated by a sense of time. It is not the way to live.

Essentially there is no such thing as time. It is only a convenience for catching planes and trains, and so on. But it is not for living, understanding, growing. If it takes a long time to do something worthwhile, well, it takes a long time. If it is worthwhile, it takes time. If it is not worthwhile, do not spend time on it.

Give children your time, your devotion, your love, your readiness to answer every question. That is what a child needs. They need the example. We do not need to give them a religion or a meditation. They are not ready for that. Give them your love.

When young children have questions about reincarnation, UFOs and so on, how much can we, their parents, tell the children, taking into account that teachers and other parents and peer groups might tell them it is rubbish? (January/February 2009)

If the parent or teacher thinks that UFOs, and so on, are rubbish, that is what they will tell them. There is nothing we can do about it, except not put them in the hands of such people.

The true answer depends very much on the age of the children. Up until six or seven years old, I do not think children should be made interested in UFOs or anything to do with what is broadly called esotericism. They should not be introduced to any religious belief or any beliefs their parents hold about esotericism. They should be allowed to grow at their own pace in their life process. Depending on who they are as souls in incarnation, that will take a longer or shorter time, but it should be left to them to create that moment. Older children from about eight to 10 to 14 should be given fairly simple answers to such questions as UFOs and reincarnation.

Reincarnation is a very difficult subject to deal with. It is one of the primary laws of our experience – the Law of Rebirth. Eventually all of us, hopefully, will know and believe sincerely, and experience directly, the truth of that law. But I would not make it known to any child under the age of six or seven.

Seven is a climactic time, a time of change, and from seven onwards some things can be offered to the child in answer to their questions but always related to the fact of the question and not as a matter of doctrinal interests of the parent. I would leave all children free from the taint of any religious or philosophical belief of the parents, free to make their own minds up in due course.

I know people who are very interested in the story of the Reappearance, of the Masters, of the return to the world of the Christ, and long to make their children from a very early age part of this story. I heard several examples of that happening, where the child began to take a very lively but completely distorted part in it. They began to get 'messages' from Masters – erroneously, of course. The Masters would not give messages to children of that age. And then the parents get in touch with me wondering whether their child has actually been the recipient of Hierarchical advice and teachings or whether they are just repeating what they had heard from the parents.

In each case, of course, they are simply repeating what they have heard from the parents, and it has been a glamour on the part of the child. Leave your children's minds alone, their belief structures alone and their religious aspirations alone, until they are old enough to make up their own minds from what they see around them. Even if it means complete denial of what their parents think. Children change.

I was raised a 'born-again' Christian, and am now a mother. For reasons of personal evolution on my part, I feel that it would be wrong to teach my children the Christianity that I was raised with, but I want to teach them something. I want to give them spiritual guidance in their lives, something that they can build on as they grow and make decisions for their future. Does Share International offer worship gatherings for families? Do you have any advice for me, on how to raise children to be progressive spiritual beings? (December 2006)

The best teaching (I think the only true teaching) is given by example. If I may dare to give you advice it would be this: give your children the gift of freedom from indoctrination and conditioning. Leave them free to be and become themselves. Keep them away from 'beliefs' and never smother their spontaneity – from it comes the expression of their uniqueness as souls.

Show them, by example, how to love people of all colours and traditions; how to be tolerant and just. Teach them, by example, the fundamental spiritual law of life, the law of Cause and Effect; in the simplest terms, "as you sow so shall you reap", and hence the need for harmlessness in all situations. Imbue them, by example, with the energy of goodwill and show them how to be relaxed and happy.

The spiritual life is not to do with beliefs and/or worship. It is the moment-to-moment sense of connection with the divine, of not being separate from that or from its expression in others. Show this, by example, to your children and they will grow as examples of that divinity before your eyes.

I have read five of your great books so far and I have several questions: (1) At what age does a child begin to accumulate karma? Does a three-year-old hurting his sister get bad karma? (2) I am diagnosed with Attention Deficit Disorder and no medication works for me (too many side effects). I have read on the Share International website that ADHD may be due to nuclear radiation and pollution. Apart from eating organic food, trying to live in a pollution-free area and doing Transmission Meditation, is there a way to cure this disease? (3) On the astral plane, you can travel where you want, as fast as you want. Are there dangerous places to go on that plane (like another planet, the sun, near a black hole, or even the black hole at the centre of the galaxy)? (July/August 2008)

(1) A child is not subject to karma until the age of 7; even then karma is mitigated to a large extent until the age of 14. (2) Not

at the present time. Until we can deal with the higher aspects of nuclear toxicity in our pollution it will not be possible to limit ADHD. I suggest using the 'Hand' of Maitreya and asking for His help.* (3) Yes, indeed. The places you suggest, black holes, etc, are not accessible on the astral planes but there are many dangers on the lower levels of the astral planes, which should not be approached without the supervision of a higher source.

[*See photograph of the 'Hand' of Maitreya in picture section]

EDUCATION OF THE YOUTH

More and more young people are lost today through depression and drugs. How can we help them? (January/February 2004)

This is a terrible problem. According to Maitreya they are suffering from spiritual starvation. The purpose and meaning of life must be restored to them. They are committing slow suicide by taking drugs, etc. They do not know about Maitreya, they do not know about the transformation of humanity which is inevitable and which will re-establish life – true life – in these young people. The way to aid them at the present moment is to tell them about the existence of Maitreya and the Masters, to show the hope that fact brings to the world, and so reinforce their self-respect. They have lost self-respect, they have lost hope. They need help from people who know better and who can help them in the way that they can understand. You must pass on the help that you receive.

A recent UK report reveals that drug use among the young is soaring despite all efforts to counter it. Can you please comment? (May 2007)

The distributors and 'pushers' of the drugs work harder than those who try to stop the distribution. They also work more systematically, and from long experience, more effectively. The educational effort is only semi-successful in preventing drug use and although widespread has not justified the time and money spent on it. The fundamental reason, however, for the increase in drugs is that through what Maitreya calls the "blind following of market forces", the government has created a condition of arid competition as the only beckoning light for young people; mostly they feel that they have nothing worthwhile to look forward to and they seek the transitory effect of drugs to alleviate their inner anxieties. They need to be given hope and sufficient inspiration to meet their innate idealism but instead they find a future empty of such inspiration. They feel at war within themselves and alienated from a society that they feel provides them with nothing worthwhile.

The growth of drug use among the young, therefore, will continue to grow in the present political economic situation. It will take Maitreya's open presence to inspire the young with the hope and enthusiasm which they have lost or have never found.

Children are getting caught up in murder and violent crime on Britain's streets – why? What has gone wrong? What can be done to tackle the causes? (October 2007)

This sad situation is not exclusive to Britain but is becoming more and more evident throughout the developed world. Through the "blind following of market forces" the politicians of the Western world have created a split society where the rich are getting richer and the poor poorer. This is very clearly the case in Britain, as in America and other 'successful' countries. These violent crimes take place primarily in the poorest areas of inner cities where children and teenagers are neglected, have no facilities for organized group play and sport, and often little or no parental guidance. They have no sense of being wanted, are alienated and at war with themselves and with the society of which they are a part. Their only family or group are the street gangs which inevitably take the place of their own. They feel that life has no meaning or hope for them and turn to violence to give it meaning. At the same time the newspapers are filled with the reports of record 'bonuses' for the heads of companies who have steered their companies to huge profits. These bonuses can be as much as £20 million a year. Is it any wonder that these children feel deprived and seek revenge?

During September and early October 2006, the US has seen a rash of school shootings involving adults going into schools and killing or wounding students or faculty. You once mentioned that where student violence is concerned it is the result of a society that teaches competition and retribution, as well as people (obviously unstable) responding to the new energies pouring into the world. Is this also a case where one act of violence 'sets off' other unstable people to act off their own ill urges? (November 2006)

Yes.

In many Western countries the incidence of depression is increasing staggeringly. In the UK, for example, the prescribing of anti-depressants has increased 700 per cent in the last 10 years. What is the reason for this 'epidemic'? (December 2002)

Depression is the social illness of a society dedicated to materialism. It is 'spiritual starvation', and is growing more and more throughout the developed Western world. The highest incidence of depression and the greatest use of anti-depressants and tranquillizers are in the USA, followed closely by Europe.

What is the effect on the younger generation who use electronic devices for many of their activities, both educational and recreational? Does this keep children in a more physical or brain state, rather than a soul intuitional state, stunting the spiritual growth of children? If so, what can be done to mitigate the effects? (March 2009)

The tools of modern life, such as electronic devices, can be either detrimental to the nervous system or extremely useful to children, in that they do not have to store so many facts in their brain. In modern education, 90 per cent of what is given are facts. These facts fill up the spaces in children's brains, especially in the developed world. Computers can store all these facts and save the brain from storing them.

There are good computers and bad computers – that is, computers that save you from storing facts, and 'toyful' computers. The use of computers for games should be limited by parents. Like many games it can become an obsession. It is like watching too much television. It is a drug that saps your energy and keeps you from experiencing the ills and fortunes of real life.

You have said that computer games can be addictive. Could the same be said about the ubiquitous use of digital music players (mp3s), and mobile phones with their myriad communication functions? Doesn't the constant distraction of pop music, text messaging, and chatting undermine the person's ability to focus and concentrate? What effects do these personal electronic devices have on the mental and spiritual development of young people? (May 2009)

All of these devices have a certain useful function. However, as widely used today, their chief effect is to divert their users from experiencing themselves and life as it is; in other words, they are an escape from reality, if overused. It will take the inspiration of Maitreya to fill young people's minds with such meaning and challenge that they no longer look for escape.

Many teenagers claim that they need a lot of sleep. Is this so? What is your Master's comment on this? (September 2002)

No. Of course, individuals vary, but most teenagers sleep long from habit and wrong eating habits. The majority should not need more than five hours sleep.

In the future will teenagers live with peers in a group setting?
(March 2009)

Some will and some will not. Some already do. It is not a particular condition that will be repeated all over the world. Some teenagers in some parts of the world, like America and Europe, will set themselves up in groups for a time perhaps. Teenagers will come to understand that they cannot develop fully by themselves and will need older people, maybe their parents or teachers of one kind or another, for input into their society. They cannot for long break away from society. Society is whole and they are part of that whole. But there will be experiments in many different directions along these lines.

Some teenagers say humanity is a virus on the Earth and should be exterminated. What would be a good response to bring in an awareness of their divinity? (January/February 2009)

Well, again it depends on the age of the teenager. A 19-year-old needs a very different answer from a 13-year-old, I would say, depending again on the point of evolution, and therefore, of the maturity of the mind of the individual.

They say it is a virus that should be eliminated and I would say: "Try it. Try to eliminate it." I think that would be enough. And if they said: "How?" I would say: "I do not know. Whatever you think." You see they would be stumped. It is only a little idea.

There are people in the world who act in a very dangerous and destructive fashion, and in the teenage phase of life people are extraordinarily aspirational. Their aspiration is fresh and new. It is coming from the heart, and they are appalled at the pain and the suffering that goes on in the world. They feel it very strongly. But to answer that cry for compassion – which it is – by the thought of annihilation of the species is just daft.

Some take up cudgels against society but also against themselves as members of that society. They feel alienated from society, rightly, because it does not do anything for them, they feel. When they look around and they see commercialization of the world, and the destructive tendencies of governments and politicians, then it is no wonder they feel like that. But because they are not very mentally developed they think annihilation will do the trick. They soon see it can't be done.

So they become more realistic and then they learn that they can influence their surroundings, and influence those they meet by their own behaviour. It is up to each one of us to be the best that we can be according to our traditions. If they are religious and want to be good Christians, well, as Maitreya would say, be the best Christian that exists, be the best Muslim, the best Hindu, the best Buddhist, or the best Jew – just be the best they can be.

There were times, as an adolescent, I would wake up in the morning and feel love in a way that I have never really felt since. I absolutely had love for everything. It was a very good feeling and I would love to live that 'state' constantly. After a few moments the feeling would dissipate, I imagine as conditioning would settle back into my consciousness. Is this an experience, somewhat at least, of living in the present moment or in the 'now'? (June 2004)

Yes. Most common among children, it tends to gradually disappear as the struggles of adolescence set in.

There has been an increase in Attention Deficit Disorder (ADD) and Attention Deficit Hyperactivity Disorder (ADHD) among our youth today in the US. (1) What is the primary cause of these disorders? (2) Does the fact that the human body now contains dozens of foreign and toxic chemicals, some that would be fatal if taken in large dosages, contribute to some of these cases? (October 2006)

(1) Pollution, especially nuclear radiation (the greatest killer). There is also the effect on many people of all ages of the heightened potencies of the new cosmic energies pouring into our planet. (2) Exactly, yes, that is the pollution I mean.

157

CHANGE IN EDUCATIONAL PROGRAMMES
AND EDUCATORS

Would you advise us as a group to develop lessons or a programme of teaching concerning the emergence of Maitreya and His teachings, and offer this to schools? (January/February 2009)

I would advise strongly the making of such programmes and offering them to the general public, not necessarily to schools. If to schools, then it would be to the higher levels. I would probably put it at 14 years and over, including, of course, universities. It would be very useful to present to the general public too. You have very little time to do it before Maitreya emerges. These questions should have been put 20 years ago and I would have given the same answers, but you would have had 20 years of practice behind you. You do not know how soon Maitreya is appearing. It is in a very, very short time.

So the answer is yes, in schools but only to the 14-year-olds and above. Only those above the age of 14 will hear the words of Maitreya telepathically on the Day of Declaration. Up until then the person is a child and that has to be respected. There is a limit to what can, or should be, given to children.

Will the changing of education happen slowly or quickly after the Day of Declaration? (January/February 2009)

For those attempting to do it, it will seem terribly slow. Change is always difficult to absorb. In education it occurs very slowly after the ideas have been debated for years, turned down and accepted, then reassessed and dropped again, all over the simplest things; and these new teachings are not simple changes. So you can expect them to seem slow.

But seen from a longer viewpoint they will be very fast indeed. There will be tremendous changes in human thought and experience even without the individual efforts of people on the ground. Radio and television will do their jobs. The internet will do its job. And people will quickly be acquainted with – and this is the point – not educated but acquainted, with the thoughts, the ideas, the concepts which relate to the new time. And once people are acquainted with the ideas they of themselves speed up or slow down the realization of them, depending on their own mental apparatus.

People in the East have known about the Law of Rebirth for thousands of years. Millions, Buddhists and Hindus, for example, take it for granted that rebirth as a doctrine is true, but they do not necessarily understand its implications. Many of them have a distorted idea of the Law of Karma – the Law of Cause and Effect – why they are poor, for instance. They think they are poor because they must have done something in a previous life to warrant it: they may have been, they think, rich but cruel and heartless, and so they are poor in this life. They do not realize poverty has a political cause. It is to do with the cause and effect of the actions of the Indian government, for example. The Indian government is making a lot of money today and India is emerging as a financial giant offering money to the West to bolster our banks so that they do not collapse, yet millions of Indians go hungry, not because of karma but because the wealth of India is not shared.

What course of action do you recommend for teachers now to fit themselves for the educational goals outlined by the Master? (March 2009)

Read more. Read as much as you can take in. The books are available, but few read them in any depth. The needs are there, but not necessarily known. So they do not arise except in a few minds. But when they arise on a broader scale, it will set up a demand for more light and therefore more experiment. Trained people will come forward and train others, who will train others, and so on. How long will it take? Who can tell?

159

How can we prepare ourselves? Read the Alice Bailey books, really study them. You can read my books if you like, but it is not for me to push them. The Alice Bailey books deal with what I think you are looking for.

Which of the Alice Bailey books do you recommend in relation to the new education? (March 2009)
I would highly recommend *Education in the New Age*. Then *Initiation, Human and Solar*. Then the books on the rays, esoteric healing, esoteric astrology. Go through them all. All of them are educational. They are given to stimulate the mind and intuition, and awaken you to levels of yourself that you may be unaware of.

For one of the subjects which I teach to groups of student teachers I ask my students to read, among other things, Krishnamurti's **Education and the Significance of Life** *(1953), which provides most relevant and practical insights into the essence of right education with regard to the needs of humanity and the world. Without fail, students complain that Krishnamurti holds very negative views of the world and humankind and that his ideas are not practical or realistic. Some will come around when I point out that his views should be applied to oneself, and that the world has not become a safer place since the Cold War, when it was first published – far from it. The other day I finally realized that perhaps because of their age (typically 22-24 years old), my students just haven't seen enough of the world yet to see the urgency of his message. Should I perhaps not bother to ask my students to read this book because of their age? Or should I continue to try to sow seeds? Your comments would be much appreciated.* (September 2008)
It takes time and concentration to get close to Krishnamurti's meaning. Keep presenting it nevertheless, and the light will dawn. These young people will soon hear Maitreya for themselves. He is Krishnamurti's mentor.

Some years ago, you said that Maitreya was training educators in London. Is that still going on? (March 2009)

As far as I know, yes. Maitreya is training educators. Some people have undergone a very simple form of training, reorientation, and certain groups have been set up in which people take over the handling of dissident school children – those who are rowdy, difficult to teach, have no goals in life. I do not know how far advanced that is. But these experiments are carried out.

The children are given a very simple breath control technique. It is designed to start a change in the direction of thinking in these alienated children. They are totally alienated from the society of which they are a part. They do not feel society has anything to give them. There are demands that they would like to make on society. They may not be able to put them into words, but they want something from society – jobs, money, freedom, justice – and they do not get any of these things. So they are seen as 'layabouts', 'no-goods', minor criminals. Maitreya has set up this simple regime with a few trained personnel who work with these young people, and in very little time change their whole viewpoint.

It begins with this breathing exercise in which they sense themselves as the Self. They do that every day, several times a day and get a stronger and stronger sense of their own identity.

Maitreya has said, "Without self esteem you can do nothing". So, what are tiny ways in which a person can increase his or her self-esteem if it is low? (June 2009)

Achievement, of any kind, in any direction, increases self-esteem. Therefore all effort should be addressed to the achieving of some goal, large or small; and then steadily 'upping' the goal, until the confidence which comes with achievement becomes steady and reliable. Aspiration is the key. If we can inspire the latent aspiration in ourselves and others, self-worth and self-esteem automatically follow.

With regard to the blueprint for educational reform, are people in the field of education being trained now just as disciples in other walks of life are trained? (January/February 2009)

In the outer world there are attempts at such reform being made here and there in different parts of the world; interestingly enough, in America probably more than elsewhere by small groups. But it is not the national policy in any country to introduce such new thought.

The first five Masters entered the everyday world in 1975, then two more and then the others. There are now 14 Masters in the world plus Maitreya. The Masters are all educators in a way. They are teachers of one kind or another, but not necessarily in a formal sense. Many of Them have other kinds of work, but the result of Their work is in the end teaching as far as we are concerned. They have given the benefit of Their teaching through Their disciples, men and women in the world. So there is a group of men and women covering the world who are now trained to be able to train others with the ideas and the formulae for a better approach to education – how it must be based on education for life.

All of this takes time. The first activity will be concerned with government, politics and so on, and only latterly education for life in that specific sense. That will be slower to implement. It has a different function even though the two functions are interrelated. But the first thing is to make sure that we do not destroy the world. So when we say we want to get rid of the atomic bomb, that has to be implemented. It has to be overseen by those whom the world can trust, which will be Hierarchy and the representatives of Hierarchy, senior disciples of Masters Who are already here.

So in the educational field, change will be slower. There are people being trained to present the big picture, the overall slant of the new education. Others can be trained to fill in the gaps and the specifics in a classroom or wherever the teaching takes place. It will not always be in a classroom; it could, for example, be in industry.

So people who work as teachers now should not try to implement their ideas about education? (January/February 2009)

No. It does not mean that at all. Any teacher worth their salt should be trying anyway to do such a thing, but it depends on the age of your pupils. Whatever you say must be adapted to the range of the minds of the children that you are dealing with. If you are dealing with young children, you should be very wary indeed of presenting to a child what becomes glamour and simply a wrong path, through an over-stimulation of the child. But for teenagers, especially above 14, by all means; they are hungry for knowledge, longing for it.

Recently, when discussing the need for education to focus on establishing right human relations, I pointed out to a younger colleague that economic values have all but replaced human values in life. To my astonishment he said he wondered if that was necessarily a bad thing, saying that the free market had brought humanity so much freedom – especially in terms of choice in products and services. I was baffled at such apparent ignorance and it left me wondering what, if anything, the Masters would say in response to such remarks? (September 2008)

They would probably say that these are not bad things to have so long as everyone has the same possibility to have them.

Being a teacher, I was wondering when we could talk openly about either the Reappearance or about the purpose of life without fear of losing our jobs? (January/February 2009)

This is a difficult question. I cannot guarantee that what I say will either ensure your job or make it absolutely certain that you are going to get the sack.

*Why does **Share International** emphasize constantly the role of people power?* (May 2003)

Because, eventually, organized, educated and inspired by Maitreya, the power of the people will manifest through a massed world public opinion against which no nation can stand. We are only at the beginning of this process but, in time, people power will be the strongest force on Earth.

People in power at present seem to be full of illusion. In what way can ordinary people like ourselves help bring about changes now? (May 2003)

Join together with groups and work to create the 'voice of the people'. Add your voice to the voice of all the other people – the ordinary people not in positions of glamorous power and illusionary wisdom. Add your weight by marching on demonstrations whenever they are arranged. Build up the concept of 'the people's voice' – which eventually will be the most powerful force in the world when it is educated by the ideas of Maitreya, focused by Maitreya, approaching the various problems of humanity in a realistic way. This will build up the most powerful force: of an educated, focused, world public opinion. Add your voice to the voices of the countless millions.

On 15 February 2003, 12.5 million people across the world marched against the war in Iraq and related issues of justice and freedom. Nearly 2 million of those (1,800,000) were in London, and they included Maitreya. He thinks it is worth joining the marches and He has joined in the demonstrations across the world. Make your voice heard. Speak out for what you believe. If you believe in justice and freedom for all – say so. Write articles and send them to the newspapers. Make known your mind on this, as your contribution to humanity's liberation from the ancient thralldom of glamour, illusion and oppression.

Remember it is humanity itself who must change the world. Maitreya comes to inspire and guide but we have to do the work.

EDUCATIONAL ROLE OF THE GROUPS

What will the role of the emergence groups be after the appearance of Maitreya? (January/February 2009)
This talk was given to show the necessity for the implementation of the work involved in what is a complete change in the view of the world. If you take seriously what is in the talk on each of the Master's three articles, 'The New Education', and education for 'The Family', and 'The Age of Light', there is an opportunity for those who fit themselves, and this is the point, who fit themselves for the task to educate a hungry public.

Those who have anything to do with the internet, who sit transfixed before that little rectangle, know that people everywhere have questions. They are filled with questions. I get questions from the public which show they have no idea of what I am really talking about and what there is on our website. But they are hungry for information of one kind or another. They are hungry to know about UFOs, for example. Are they real? Where do they come from? What is their function? What is their role? Are they friendly? Are they aggressive? People are hungry for information. And so there is work for everybody who wants to do it – to present our information in a sane and level-headed way, with a knowledgeable view of the new time, the new forms of government, of education, and technology. There is a vast field of service.

I gave this talk to emphasize how short a time it is until Maitreya comes into the world and therefore how really short a time it is until the Day of Declaration, when there will be an enormous demand for knowledge. Any group connected with this work will become a centre for information. You are all from different groups, different countries, but it is to those groups who have become known for giving talks, for putting up information in libraries and so on, for publishing books, that the public will turn. You will become known for being the only people approachable in your area or your country for this information.

Now, don't think you can phone me for all the answers to questions from the public! I am not going to answer your public through you. You have to acquaint yourself with the information. Read the books; the more you read the books, the more you will know. I wonder how many of you have actually read the books. I think it is rare indeed, judging by the questions I am asked!

What will be the relationship between the emerging Masters and the Share International group in this role as teachers and educators? (March 2009)
It depends on what you make of it. The Masters coming out are not all doing the same work. They are very specialized. Sometimes the specialties overlap, but They all have Their own line of work, Their own group of disciples. The Masters will work with their immediate disciples. They may be in any department – politics, education or whatever.

Those involved in education may or may not work with people in this group. This group knows, or somewhat knows, certain things that other groups do not know. Just by having done this work, they have come to somewhat understand some of the esoteric ideas. They can do a tremendous service in bringing a range of knowledge to the general public about the true constitution of man, the purpose of life, the nature of the soul, and so on. There are thousands of questions one could answer which will be asked. The public will want to know. The Share International website will be red hot, bursting with questions, which already come from the public.

These questions need answers, and I cannot be the only one who answers them. Everyone at this conference today, for example, could answer a lot of the questions that come. That is a field of service in itself.

Does the process of formulating ideas and presenting them to the public in the form of **Share International** *magazine, for example, have a positive influence not only on those who read the magazine but also, less directly, on the mental planes by a sort of passing on of the thoughtforms?* (August 2003)
Yes, precisely so.

How can we inspire others in an educational exchange? (January/February 2009)
Well, first of all smile; smile and look brisk and very much energized by the whole proceeding. That is the major thing. They will say: "He or she obviously knows all the answers. Thank goodness, because I do not. Now inspire me." When the smile is getting a bit painful to maintain, do not let it drop, keep it up at all costs. Keep your smile up. And then you can nod your head up and down – yes, yes. If you can get your head to nod while you are talking, underlining that what you are saying is true, then they will be inspired. They will understand you are a very inspiring person. And you can raise your voice when it seems meaningful to do so, and if you can get a kind of thrill in it, an underlying thrill in the voice that what you are saying is especially important, and especially true, and very, very esoteric, it will be inspiring. That is really the only answer I can give. Just joking!

Seriously, the way to inspire people is to believe it yourself. You cannot inspire people if you do not believe. But if you do believe it, it is easy. You just tell them. Just be yourself, don't exaggerate. The truth of the story itself is inspiring – if people are ready for it.

How do we prepare ourselves to discern the nature of a child, as in ray structure and point of evolution? (March 2009)

There are two books by Alice Bailey on the rays (*A Treatise on the Seven Rays, Part One* and *Two*). Study them, really study them, for years. People read a book in a couple of weeks and then do their ray structure. Of course, they are all wrong. What can they learn in two weeks? You get to know the rays and it becomes an instinct. You could usefully study the list of rays given, for example, in my book, *Maitreya's Mission, Volume Three*.

How long do you estimate it will be before the ray structure, point of evolution and soul purposes of the world's students are known? By what mechanism will this occur? Who will be trained to reveal them and how? (March 2009)

Not until the Masters are out in the world and their disciples are trained to recognize and read the ray structures, point of evolution, and soul purposes. What is the main purpose of this child's soul, as exemplified in its ray structure? All of that needs trained people to determine, which the Masters' disciples will train people to do.

The Masters, of course, can do it, but They will not take on all the world's students. At the very most there will only be about 40 Masters, plus Maitreya, eventually in the world. There will be 14 for the present, plus Maitreya. I do not know when more will come in. It will depend on the extent to which humanity sets up the evocative desire, when we have put into place what we can put into place ourselves, when we have learned what we can learn, when we have been trained as far as we can be trained. Then more Masters will come in as more demand is set up. Nothing is withheld that can be released safely to humanity. We ourselves limit that possibility by the nature of our receptivity and our readiness for more knowledge.

Can you talk about a 3rd-ray mind? (March 2009)

At its highest, the 3rd ray is the Ray of Higher Abstract Mind, reflective and creative. The 3rd-ray mind finds the outer, form aspect easy to deal with and control. It is the ray of philosophy and higher teaching. It is also the ray of adaptability. The 3rd-ray mind finds the form aspect easy to deal with and control.

The glamours of the 3rd-ray mind can make it manipulative and unprincipled, the 'spider at the centre of the web' in touch with everyone and pulling the strings of everyone in the group. It longs to control everyone in its orbit. It brings people together who should not be together. It keeps people apart who should be together. It manipulates these pieces in its environment and feels central to it all. It likes to be in touch with everyone, to be the one who knows what everyone is doing, thinking and feeling, marshalling them into confrontation. It likes to be in control. It can also handle the truth with less than care and does not hesitate to lie to gain a point. Such are the glamours of the 3rd-ray mind.

The combination of that with the glamours of the 6th ray make, in my opinion, the worst combination – the Milosevics of the world. Milosevic came in as a communist, giving the world to the people, but took everything from the people for himself, his wife and his party, and sent his forces into Bosnia and Herzegovina as soon as Tito died.

How can we best serve in a world with so much poverty and degradation? (March 2009)

There are 6.5 or so billion people in the world, too many by far. This world can easily hold about 4-5 billion people and will eventually arrive at that number. There are many more people in this world than the planet needs or can conveniently support. However, there is more food and raw materials in the world than we need. It is simply not distributed.

If you were to live in Mexico City, for example, which has about 22-24 million people, you would be aware that there are too many people. Most of the people in Mexico City live in the outskirts, which go on forever. The people there are so poor, so destitute. Their buildings are shanty towns.

Driving to the airport, you have to stop at a traffic light. People immediately come up to the car selling roses or last year's lottery tickets. One little girl who has nothing to sell does cartwheels in front of the car. It is the only thing she can think to do just for a few pesos. This in a city with rich hotels and rich people.

I remember an old woman sitting on a bench on a bit of dirty green grass outside a church, which was closed. She sat on the bench because it happened to be there. It was well back from the pavement. People passed on the pavement but not near her. She had a small bathroom scale at her feet so that people passing could stop and have their weight taken and give her a few pesos for the trouble. Of course, they just passed by. No one had their weight taken. No one touched the scale. They did not even see it. That was all she had to sell, a bathroom scale, hoping someone might stop and have their weight taken.

The poverty is so heartbreaking. There is also the terrible mound of waste material on the outskirts of Mexico City, which burns day and night. Hundreds of people make their living out of sorting out the little saleable items from the garbage. We published an article on this in *Share International* in the early days.

When the world's resources are at last shared, and peace and justice are facts of life, many avenues of service and of knowledge will open up before those who are willing and anxious to serve. Meanwhile, the bringing of sanity and justice to the world is the number one priority and there are many open doors for people who truly want to serve.

(1) Many in the groups are interested in healing, but no specific instruction has been given about it. Is that because the primary task, at least initially, is educational? (2) Will the Masters be

*giving training in healing? (3) Would that be in some years'
time?* (December 2002)

(1) Partly, yes. (2) Not directly, but through disciples. (3) Yes.

*(1) Why are some countries more prone to paranoia than others?
(2) What makes certain populations more easily manipulated
than others?* (June 2004)

(1) Nations are at various degrees of maturity as nations and so
their people have more or less maturity of vision, tolerance,
understanding and grasp of the need for co-operation among
nations and respect for the rule of law in international affairs.
(2) Where less emphasis is given to education and the upholding
of the democratic principle, the ability of a government to
manipulate the population is increased. Manipulation through a
controlled media is, of course, one of the most dangerous (and
effective) means used by governments today.

FAMILY AND KARMA

*(1) Is it true that some people are not related by karma to their
immediate families? (2) If so, why does this happen? (3) If we
are not related by karma to our direct relatives (parents and
siblings) does that make family life more difficult? Would there
be less mutual understanding in such circumstances? (4) Are we
not generally born in groups? (5) The notion seems strange
since you would share genetic material but have no 'past' in
common.* (November 2007)

(1) Yes, it is relatively rare but it occurs. (2) It is the action of the
life, which has many mysteries. It brings into an incarnating
group a new and different energy or stimulus and prepares the
way for some soul-envisaged purpose. (3) Not necessarily. (4)
Yes, but a group is a dynamic process. (5) Life is very inventive
and creative.

If karma is so important in terms of families, what about adoption? Who should raise orphans? (March 2009)

Orphans should only be adopted by those who have the capacity to give a child a stable background with a mother and father, the love which it needs, and the wisdom and lack of conditioning that most children hopefully receive from their parents. That is asking for the ideal. All people are conditioned because they are the children of people who are themselves conditioned by their parents. Parents pass on to their children their glamours, prejudices, hopes and fears. The children are brought up under the constraints of these fundamental fears and glamours of their parents. That goes for adopted children as well.

The alternative for many adopted children is going to an orphanage, where they are usually one among a large group of similarly abandoned or neglected children. They are brought up together by people who often have very little love, very little opportunity even to learn how to look after children and bring them up sanely and lovingly, as they need.

If it is a question of adoption into a family or living in an institution, nine times out of ten, I would say a family. With all its faults, the family is absolutely the best unit in which to bring up a child. In an adopted family there would not be the karmic situation that is usually there in a birth family. There would not be the ties and knots that have to be untied and resolved, which the family unit gives the opportunity to do. But in an adopted family there could be, and hopefully would be, the love, concern, and the trust that can be developed through love, and a sane uncompetitive treatment of the child.

To be part of a larger family where there are two or three other children probably is the best situation. That provides most of what the child would need. It might be better to be alone with the parents, perhaps in the beginning, but not for long. To be part of a larger family that is already happy and established, and presents a wholesome view to the incomer who is loved and received openly by the children of the new family, would probably be the best.

We have questions for your Master about adoption of children. 'Adoption' in the following questions means: a) the adoption of children by a married childless couple; b) adoption of children by a married couple with their own children; c) adopting the partner's child from a former relationship. (1) What does the Hierarchy think about adoption of children in general? (2) Is there a difference between these three different forms of adoption? (November 2007)

(1) Hierarchy is very much in favour of the adoption of parentless children. They are not in favour of the adoption by relatively rich people in the West of poor children who are not parentless, from other, mainly Eastern countries. (2) Basically not, although each situation could be different.

Is adoption an inadmissible intervention in the life of a child with disadvantageous consequences for the child? (November 2007)

Not usually.

(1) If a couple adopt a child, should the parents have the same country of origin as the child that they want to adopt? (2) Is it all right that they have different nationalities of origin? (3) What does the Hierarchy think about adoption of children with other races than the parents? (November 2007)

(1) Not important. (2) Yes. (3) It is acceptable if the other requirements of adoption are met.

(1) What is the best age of the child for adoption? (2) From which age upwards should the child not be adopted? (November 2007)

(1) As young as possible. (2) Above 14 it is usually too late for the child to bond fully, but this need not rule out adoption.

Which requirements should parents meet for an adoption of a child? (November 2007)

If they can give love and protection to the child as if she/he were their own.

What is the attitude of Hierarchy to adoption by gay couples and single people? (November 2007)

Hierarchy knows that adoption by gay couples and single people often results in a perfectly happy outcome for both child and parents. However from the point of view of Hierarchy only a stable heterosexual couple can provide ideal role models for the growing child.

In the article 'The Family', is the Master talking more about homosexuals creating a child by artificial insemination than about such a couple adopting an otherwise unwanted child? Or are both actions unhelpful? (March 2009)

He is talking about both. Male homosexuals cannot have a child. They have to adopt. Female homosexuals can have a child by artificial insemination. The Master is talking about both cases because neither couple provides the necessity of mother and father. It is true to say that many homosexual couples who, by either method – adoption or artificial insemination – have children and look after them, do so with complete love and kindness, thinking only of the child's well-being. But in principle, it is unhelpful to the child because of the lack of a male and female person with whom to develop his or her own emotional structure. In either case, there would be no karmic tie necessarily. There might be, but there might be no known karmic tie to bring the child and parents together.

Generally speaking, it is unhelpful for the race as a whole and for the development of the race in relation to the Plan. The Master is always talking in relation to the Plan. The Plan is set and the Masters are its Custodians. The Plan is in the mind of the

Logos of the planet. The Masters are the only people in the world Who really know the Plan. Some of Their immediate disciples may have a good idea of the Plan, but the Masters are the only ones Who know the Plan of the Logos. That is Their total concern. Everything is geared to the furtherance of the Plan. In this case, it is doing what is best for the child and the race in accordance with the tenets of the Plan. People tend not to take that into account, but the Masters absolutely do. They see homosexual relationships in relation to adoption or artificial insemination as unhelpful to the Plan.

I know your Master's article about children and gays is a lot deeper and more helpful to all than I understand at my point of evolution, but I'd like to know more about how to handle the criticism of readers who misinterpret it as bigotry. (December 2002)

The Master's article is not about "children and gays" but about the family unit as the basic form in which children can find the necessary relationships to evolve correctly from an esoteric and karmic standpoint. The Master says expressly that Hierarchy is not the enemy of homosexuals, but it is obvious that single-sex partnerships cannot provide the full requirements for children's inner development. I have no doubt that same-sex partners can and do provide, to adopted children, the love and care which all children need.

If we suffer hardships in this life is it because we have done wrongs in our past lives and have not learned from experience? (September 2008)

Yes, usually but not always. For example, there is general world or group karma to which we are all subject. What we experience as hardship is also relative; to some people it would seem like nearly heaven.

If we do not have memories of our past lives and what we did, how are we ever going to evolve as better human beings and help humanity? (September 2008)

It is a question of aspiration, not of the memory of past lives. Experience eventually comes to everyone, whether we remember or not. If people have the aspiration to better themselves and the world so much the better. It is nothing to do with memory; we are what we are.

Nowadays there are a lot of young people who do not get married. Is there a spiritual reason for this tendency? (July/August 2006)

Only occasionally is there a spiritual reason why people do not get married or should not have children. But it is only very occasional. Marriage is a social institution – because society used to demand it. Nowadays, and in some societies, this is changing and people live together and also have children out of wedlock.

I think there are several reasons. One is the change in social mores. Young people are born free – they don't feel the restrictions of the past and the social pressures.

Spiritual marriage is something different from a contract signed in a registry office. Religions emphasize the necessity of marriage. Many spiritually-minded people do not get married. Many people get divorced, so many young people decide not to get married. If people are living together as husband and wife and do not plan to have children I don't think it matters very much. But if they plan to have children it is better to get married for the sake of the children, even if it is difficult; if a couple are not married but have children it is easier for them to separate. It is better for children to have both a mother and a father figure to relate to so that they grow up with a balanced psychological attitude to themselves and the sexual problems they may meet.

Everybody has five levels on which they have to meet their partner – at present it is very haphazard. True spiritual marriage has to meet correctly on the soul level, personality, mental, emotional and physical levels. Who has that? One in millions, probably – where people meet who were related in past lives, perhaps, on these levels. In future, as the right education permeates through humanity, more truly spiritual marriages will be formed through right identity on all levels. If people have right relationship on more than one level today, it is a kind of miracle. This is all part of the new education and new psychology.

I fear for the grief I will have to deal with when my sisters or my parents go to the astral plane. I will miss them terribly. I comfort myself by saying: "I will see them again when I go there myself." However, what if they have incarnated back on the physical plane again before I have had a chance to see them? Will I be doomed to never see them again? Can you help me with this? Please be compassionate in your response. (March 2009)

Don't despair, we incarnate in groups, changing relationships again and again. You could be the father of your parents and sisters or in some other relationship.

MAKING KNOWN THE HARM OF POLLUTION

When will the harmful aspect of nuclear radiation be revealed? (January/February 2009)

I reveal it in practically every lecture I give, every time I open my mouth, in every book I write, every time I hear about new power stations or the growth of nuclear power to overcome global warming. If the world had listened to us, it would have known over the last, some 30 years that nuclear radiation is bad for you. It should not be taken by mouth! In fact it should not be taken at all because the most harmful aspect of nuclear radiation is above the level that our present day technology can measure. They do not even understand that there are levels of radiation which they cannot measure. I have been saying that for years, have I not? They just will not listen.

So it is not a revelation we are waiting for. I think the question should really be when would the information be heeded? That probably depends on Maitreya. People will ask Maitreya about the dangers or otherwise of nuclear power stations and He will give the correct answer, no doubt. So, like a great many other things, it probably depends on Maitreya.

If the dangers of nuclear radiation on the etheric level cannot be measured, how can we influence politicians of the need to discontinue nuclear power stations? (March 2009)
How do you get anything done in this country? You have to protest. So many people have to talk about it that the politicians take note. They may not believe a word of what you say, but they have to take note.

When Maitreya starts speaking openly, He will talk about this. In answer to questions, He will say very clearly that the plans for building dozens of nuclear power stations throughout the world must be abandoned. It is not the way of the future. It is dangerous and harmful to humanity and the lower kingdoms.

You will be stimulated to take action. As soon as you hear this growing concern about nuclear power, add your voice. March and demonstrate, write in to the newspapers, magazines and blogs, and make it known.

Humanity is powerful. It has no idea of its power. There is nothing more powerful than a properly educated massed public opinion. Maitreya counts on the formation of that mass public opinion to overthrow the present commercialization and to bring in the principles of sharing and justice. We owe it to ourselves to do it. No one else is going to do it. You know about it, so you can start the ball rolling. It will not roll by itself. I am telling you what I know, but it is generally unknown. I have ways and means of getting information and passing it on to you. You pass it on to those who need to know, and on and on, and build up a barrier to any future use of nuclear radiation, power stations and all the rest. The danger of the higher levels of radiation is only one factor. I just mentioned the worst, but all the factors concerning nuclear power are dangerous.

Would it be beneficial to take a homoeopathic remedy for radiation? Is there another antidote to help or are we stuck with it until we can get it out of our atmosphere? (March 2009)

The Space People are doing their best within the karmic law to neutralize the effects of nuclear radiation. That is a tremendous help. The Masters also have the ways and means of neutralizing the effects of nuclear radiation, but until They are working openly in the world, They are not going to be much involved in that. There is already a liaison between our Masters and the Space People, especially from Mars and Venus. They are working out ways and means of neutralizing more radiation within the karmic law. At the moment they are conditioned by the karmic law.

Ways and means will open as the Space Brothers become more acceptable to humanity, as the idea of their presence grows, and they are acknowledged to be really here and helping humanity. That is instead of being presented, as they are, by the governments, especially the US government, as totally degenerate, alien beasts who have their claws in humanity. It is a terrible calumny against the Space Brothers to whom we owe a great karmic debt.

There is no remedy for radiation that I know but people whose bodies are affected by radiation can go to a homoeopath. It depends on the homoeopath. If you have a homoeopath who can make a particular vaccine for you that can be fed back to you, you could probably get rid of a large amount of the nuclear radiation. It can be done, but you have to be very clever in a homoeopathic sense and know what you are doing in an

179

energetic sense. I do not know if such people exist in this country [USA].

I do not know the full answer to this question. But I know this will be discovered and developed in a mass sense. It is possible by homoeopathy to rid the body of the higher radiation that we are talking about.

Can taking homoeopathic Tlacote Water tablets* neutralize the effects of nuclear radiation? (March 2010)

To a certain extent, yes. What it does is strengthen your immunity and whatever strengthens your immunity will strengthen your ability to resist the effect of nuclear radiation. The Tlacote tablets work directly on the cells of the body and they remake all the cells, renew the cells. The cells as you know are changing all the time. They are dying and being remade over and over again every few weeks and months. The regular taking of the Tlacote or Nordenau tablets helps this process, which is the immunization of the physical body.

[*Maitreya appeared miraculously 'out of the blue' at an open-air prayer/healing meeting in Nairobi, Kenya, on 11 June 1988. He was photographed addressing (in their own language) six thousand people who instantly recognized Him as the Christ. The story and photographs were reported by major media including CNN. Similar events were witnessed by groups of all religious faiths around the world. At the same time, water sources were charged by Maitreya in the near vicinity. These miraculous healing waters have so far been discovered in Mexico, India and Germany. A total of 777 water sources will eventually be found. Water from Mexico (Tlacote) and Germany (Nordenau), with healing properties energized by Maitreya, are available in homoeopathic remedies.]

There is a lot of pollution about. Is using homoeopathic remedies, like "Air Pollution" tablets good? Could you end up causing the symptoms, if you over-use the remedy? (January/February 2008)

I would certainly recommend homoeopathic remedies for the effects of pollution. A basic rule in homoeopathy is that if taking a remedy is too prolonged it can produce the symptoms it is trying to cure. So it requires proper timing and common sense.

What did you have in mind when you talked about karmic debt regarding nuclear pollution? (January/February 2009)

We owe the Space Brothers, from Mars and Venus in particular, an enormous karmic debt. They are neutralizing not only nuclear radiation but also the effects of great toxic gases and chemicals which we spew into our atmosphere, and which make breathing on planet Earth a problem. It would probably be very difficult indeed to live on this planet but for the work of the Space Brothers neutralizing, to a large extent, the worst impact of these nefarious toxic gases and fumes and vaporized liquids which we pour daily, hourly into our atmosphere, into the ground and the oceans.

So that means that we owe them a karmic debt. From the Masters' point of view, pollution is the number one killer in the world. It breaks down our immune system, and leaves us open to all kinds of disease.

THE TECHNOLOGY OF LIGHT

Is autism caused by nuclear radiation? Can autism and Alzheimer's and other radiation-related diseases be cured or are these people destined to live with these conditions for the rest of their lives? (January/February 2009)

Autism is not always, but often, the result of nuclear radiation in the atmosphere. Can it be cured? At the present time, no. In the future, hopefully yes, or to some degree, and Alzheimer's similarly, with the Technology of Light. This means, not immediately but some time ahead, with an advanced form of genetic engineering and the energy of light available through the Technology of Light, people will go into a clinic for a few hours and come out again with a healing of the brain. What happens in Alzheimer's is that the brain actually physically shrinks, so there is less and less brain matter to create the connections that make our responses. In the new time, it will occur less frequently and only later in life.

In the clinics of the future, the relationship between the Technology of Light and an advanced form of genetic engineering will mean that we can have renewed hearts, livers, kidneys, different organs of the body in just a few hours. So even the most advanced surgery of the present will be made redundant and people find themselves completely cured with new parts to the body depending on the need. Transplants will become unnecessary. It will take time but there is a positive outlook for both Alzheimer's and autism.

In other cases, autism is frequently the result of a soul limitation of its vehicle. The soul has purposes life after life and if it sees that the personality is not carrying out any of the soul's purpose then it might in the next life limit its apparatus. So it might be an autistic or a Down's Syndrome child or have some limitation, physical or mental. In the following life, after that period of limitation, the person would be renewed in their impulse to life and would make good progress from then on. Today we do not know if we are dealing with the results of pollution or of karmic limitation – which is one and which is the other? It takes a Master to tell.

Could you say something about the positive use of atomic energy, for example, in the medical field? (January/February 2009)

Today the energy of the atom is used in the treatment for instance of cancer but it is a very clumsy process that kills the tissues as well as the tumour. This will be superseded by the science of the Technology of Light and genetic engineering.

Wilhelm Reich (1897-1957) discovered etheric matter many years ago but was rejected by society. Will this work be acknowledged in time to save the planet from the effects of nuclear radiation on the etheric planes? Will etheric matter be rediscovered? How will science find out about etheric pollution? (March 2009)

In his experiments, Wilhelm Reich discovered what esotericists know as the higher levels of etheric matter. Reich was a scientist, not an esotericist. He was not looking for the etheric, but that was the result of the experiments. He saw that there is a primordial energy in every aspect of matter, whatever form it takes. He called it 'orgone'.

Society did not reject Reich. Society did not know much about him. The US Food and Drug Administration rejected him. He was imprisoned for creating instruments, in this case boxes called 'orgone accumulators', purporting to store and use a 'non-existent' energy in a medical situation. To the Food and Drug officers orgone did not exist because they did not know about it. He knew about it from his experiments.

Reich saw orgone as one plane of energy that is everywhere. I would call it the higher etheric levels of matter. There are four planes rather than one plane of energy.

Reich was absolutely correct in his experimentation. There are many experiments which prove the existence of orgone. Reich offered to repeat those experiments before his accusers, the Food and Drug Administration, on condition that he would conduct the experiments, so there would be no tampering with the technology. The experiments are repeatable. He offered to conduct them and was rejected. Reich died in prison. He was a great man, totally unacknowledged, a second-degree initiate when he died. Will his work be acknowledged in the future? I am sure it will.

I made an orgone accumulator at home in 1948 and I know other people who have made them. I know of a man who made an orgone room or, rather, an 'esoteric room', in such a way that it attracts the energy from the four etheric planes. The orgone accumulator that I made attracts the fourth and third etheric. The levels attracted depend on the materials used. When in nature you find an underlying principle, whether by intuition or experiment, you realize how simple everything in nature really is.

For example, the new Science of Light, that will be given to humanity when we have relinquished war and all the horrors of our modern economic and political systems, is basically simple. But we have to understand the principle. With that, the actual technical process is safe and relatively simple.

According to **New Scientist** *magazine, scientists have discovered that space is filled by an unknown radiation. Its radiation is six times stronger than all known astronomic sources within this frequency band taken together. The scientists were seeking to discover small changes in the cosmic background frequency, the microwave echo of the Big Bang. Instead they discovered something more exciting: a mysterious radiation, whose origin is absolutely unclear, which seems to fill the universe. The astronomers believe that they have discovered something new: according to the NASA scientists involved, the signal was not discovered earlier since Earth-based telescopes were not yet sensitive enough. What is it? Please could you comment on this discovery?* (January/February 2009)

If the scientists are representing correctly what they are seeing, they are discovering for themselves what has already been discovered by Wilhelm Reich, who discovered a primordial energy he named 'orgone'. He saw it as an energy that interpenetrated all forms of matter. He experimented with orgone in many ways: in healing and cloud-busting (making rain) where and when needed, by very simple means.

I believe that the vibration which astronomers have discovered – the 'orgone' of Wilhelm Reich – and the higher etheric levels of matter, are one and the same. Scientists today recognize matter as being solid, liquid and gaseous but esotericists know that there are four further states of matter above gas known as the 4th, 3rd, 2nd and 1st planes of etheric matter. So instead of three planes, there are actually seven planes of matter.

All matter is a precipitation of light and so the field of matter is light precipitated into seven more or less material planes.

CROP CIRCLES

Why do the Space Brothers create crop circles? (July/August 2004)

The crop circles are created by people mainly from Mars and Venus and with a few exceptions from other planets. The majority are in the south of England but they have been seen all around the world. Our planet, like all planets, has a magnetic field; its magnetic energy travels in lines and criss-crosses, and where these lines cross is formed, eventually, a vortex, a force centre. The space people, in making the crop circles, are replicating on the dense-physical plane these magnetic vortices in our planetary magnetic field. So there is the planetary magnetic field on its own level, and then a physical plane counterpart of that, which is being replicated by the space people who are manning the UFOs, and creating the crop circles.

They do this in order to make the foundation on the physical plane for a new type of energy and a new type of technology using that energy, which eventually will be developed on this planet. It is a gift for this coming time, the New Age of Aquarius which we are entering, a time in which tremendous new discoveries in the use of the energy of the planet and the sun will be found and adopted. This will entirely change our way of life on this planet, and will lead to a control of universal energy such as we cannot begin to imagine.

In the next 2,500 years we will reach a stage where we can travel around our solar system at will, and out into the galaxy, exploring first our own solar system and then the vast galactic area, using energy which does not work within the time/space reality. People think that if you are going to send something into the galaxy, it will take hundreds of years, the people would die before they could reach anywhere that was worth going to, and they would never return. It is not true. People come here from Mars and Venus in minutes. It does not take time, once you understand that time does not exist and that the space which you thought you have to cover to get from one place to another does not exist either, and in minutes you can travel vast distances in space.

Why did they choose crops for showing these patterns?
(July/August 2004)
Crop circles are used because they are seasonal. The crops only have a short life cycle and then they are cut down, so you no longer see the crop circles. They grow up again the following year, and the crop circles appear in the same places, because they are recreated each time in the exact same point, so that the energy is put in that field, or whatever. This is a tangential way, without infringing our free will, of telling the people of Earth that the Space Brothers, the people from other planets like Mars and Venus, are here, are part of our system and that they work in a systemic way, not just as separate planets. They are helping this planet to develop the technology of the future, and also to make known, quietly, that they are helping us and that they are 100 per cent friendly and harmless.

It is very difficult to believe in the true nature of the crop circles, because there are so many hoaxes. Could you tell me what percentage of crop circles are genuine and how many are hoaxes? And why are people doing this? (July/August 2004)

There are, of course, some hoaxes but these are a tiny minority, perhaps 4 per cent, of the real and authentic crop circles which appear all over the world. The ratio of hoaxes to authentic ones varies from country to country. In this country [UK] – because we have had so many crop circles for so long – they are probably a bigger percentage than elsewhere. And in other parts of the world perhaps there is not such a conscious involvement of people with the crop circles, so they do not take the trouble to make them. To make a crop circle is hard work, and they are usually very obvious and very clumsy and badly made. How anyone can mistake a hoax for a real crop circle – if they visit the actual crop circles – astonishes me, because they are so perfectly made when they are authentic.

They are enormous yet made in seconds by the people using the space vehicle. First, they decide what the design will be. It may be very simple, and if you follow the sequence of crop circles, you see that they become more and more elaborate, more complex, as the years go on. First, for variety, and secondly, to show a complexity and a degree of ingenuity and design which would be beyond the range of any hoaxer.

The hoaxes are usually very elementary, rather badly made. Why are they made? I would say, for two reasons. One is that they are made by people who are paid to make hoaxes. Newspapers, for example, do from time to time put up money and employ, say, a group of university students who have worked out a way in which you can make a crop circle of a kind, a rather simplistic kind, but one that would convince a journalist. Journalists know no more about crop circles than the average person in the street, and yet they come along with their cameras and look at it, and they say: "Yes, it is a crop circle, a real authentic crop circle, how wonderful!" and then Doug and Dave, or Willy and Robert, come up and say: "No, we made it, yesterday, we made it! The *Daily Mail* or *The Sun* paid us £2,000 to make this crop circle, we can prove it. This is a complete hoax, they are all hoaxes." It is a way of diminishing the value and the reality of the crop circles.

Also, I know for certain, that the Ministry of Defence in this country pays money to the farmers to cut down the crop circles if they appear in their corn. Some of them, of course, go ahead and as soon as a circle appears they cut it down. Even if the corn is not ripe and they would not normally cut down that area of corn for perhaps a few weeks or a month. And so you see fields with a great hole in the middle of the corn, which is where there has been a crop circle deliberately destroyed by the farmer – paid by the Ministry of Defence.

A crop circle appeared one week ago in Winchester which is quite elaborate – a three-dimensional picture of a Hollywood-style head of an alien. You said that it was man-made which astonishes me, because you can't really recognize it from the ground. How can an ordinary person actually distinguish what is genuine and what not? (July/August 2004)

It can be difficult for people who are not to some degree well acquainted with the subject, to tell the difference between a true, authentic crop circle, made by a spaceship from Mars or Venus, and one that is just a fake. But if you have been looking at them over a period of time, and have realized the differences, you can see instantly that this is a fake and this is authentic, they are very clear cut. I saw the Winchester photograph: there is a circle in which the spaces are divided into squares in both ways, it makes a kind of a cake, but decorated in squares, and near it a head, a kind of imaginary alien's head, a head which is used every time a comic artist wants to design a spaceman, rather like the head of E.T. That to me is a complete fake. It has nothing to do with the crop circle beside it, which is authentic.

Some people simply like to play pranks, they like to destroy evidence, they like to be cleverer than those who are making the crop circles – until the public and the media cannot make head or tail of the whole thing. It destroys the credibility of the whole crop circle phenomenon. If you cannot tell the difference between a fake one and an authentic one, then the authentic ones lose credibility. Not ultimately, but for the present time until it is proved that crop circles are, indeed, made by UFOs from Mars and Venus. The number of fakes is really very small, because they are difficult to do, they take time and energy, and people who are going to spend that time and energy either have an overdeveloped sense of humour or else they are being paid to do it. Both things happen.

Just to get it clear about that Winchester crop circle: the disk is genuine? (July/August 2004)
For the one I saw in the newspaper, the actual circle is genuine but the head of an 'E.T.' is not authentic; it is a man-made one to nullify the validity of the other.

The crop circle phenomenon started to appear in the late 1970s, but even before, in the 15th or 16th centuries, people knew about them. Why are they appearing in such numbers now, and why mainly, as it seems, in the UK? (July/August 2004)
The number of crop circles is increasing all over the world. They have always been there, but only in small numbers. They are increasing because the plan of the Space Brothers – in relation to the Spiritual Hierarchy of our planet – is to speed up the creation of this magnetic field of energy on the physical plane on the Earth to do with the coming technology. Why now? Because the whole process is speeding up. Because our own Spiritual Hierarchy is returning to the everyday world.

Could you say a few words on the energy in crop circles? Is it good to stay in a crop circle for healing, for example?

The crop circles are made by energy. The people in the spaceship form a design in their mind, simple or complex, and then, with a combination of technology and thought, that design is created in the crop.

They always use a universal system based on '9', rather than '10', which we will adopt in the future. When we understand the nature of the mathematical ratios in the true sense, we will begin to understand the crop circles better. Many people think crop circles are ideograms – which they are not. They are not giving us ideas, encapsulating ideas. They are designs, carried out to a certain formula, and the formula is universal. That is what they are reiterating over and over again in these designs.

In every case there is an energy which is embedded in the ground, in the water, etc, wherever the crop circle is made. You must understand that the crop circles are only external visible points where these vortices occur. The vortices occur all over the world, even where there are no crops. So there are thousands of these energy points, vortices, created by the Space Brothers. When they make a vortex in a crop you see it as a circle; when they make it in the ocean you do not see it, but it is there, too.

In this way they are forming a magnetic grid that will be a source of energy on the physical plane, like storage tanks of energy. So it will draw energy from our own magnetic field, but using it on the physical plane in the coming technology. In using energy from the sun in relation to this magnetic energy we will do wonders in healing, in transport and many other ways; all our energy needs will be met.

If you go to a crop circle and you are sensitive to the energy, you will find that they feel different. One made by a Venusian spaceship will be quite distinct from one made by a Martian spaceship. If it is made by a Mercury or Jupiterian spaceship it will be different again.

These energies can be felt and can heal but they are not specifically of a healing nature. I would not recommend spending a lot of time in a crop circle, because one can be overcharged by the energy, especially Venusian energy, which is very high in vibration. So I recommend care in spending time in crop circles. Spend maybe five or 10 minutes in it, but not a couple of hours talking with people, and so on. People do this, and then wonder why they are so overcharged.

It has been suggested that the UK crop circle patterns have a common mathematical root in the 'golden mean'. Is this theory correct? (October 2001)
No, it has no bearing on the design of the circles, which is more arbitrary but creative and spontaneous than you might imagine.

What is the relationship between the world grid which the Space Brothers are using to prepare for the Technology of Light, and the Planetary Etheric web which Shamballa, Hierarchy and humanity are concerned with? (September 2008)
There is no real relationship except through the Law of Correspondence.

PATTERNS OF LIGHT

(1) Can it be taken for granted that most circles or patterns of light appearing increasingly all over the world are all made either by Maitreya and the Space Brothers or by Maitreya? (2) If one stands on the spot where the sun and reflected light create a circle of light can one feel the energy? (3) Is there energy radiating from such light shapes? (4) Are they healing energies? (March 2002)
(1) They are created by the Space Brothers in association with Maitreya. (2) No. (3) Yes, light energy. (4) No, not necessarily on an individual physical level but they have a 'healing dimension' in a planetary sense.

191

(1) How long have these patterns of light existed? (2) Is a reflection necessary for the creation of a circle of light (for example the reflection of a window)? (3) Is sunlight necessary for its creation? (4) What is the purpose of the patterns of light? (5) Different forms have been discovered. Do they have a symbolic meaning? (6) Will there be more forms in the future? (March 2002)

(1) About four to five years. (2) Yes. (3) Yes. (4) They are signs – miracles without religious meaning. (5) No. (6) Yes.

(1) Are the light patterns energized in any way by Maitreya or the Space Brothers and, if so, with what types of energy? (2) Do the light patterns have healing properties? (October 2001)

(1) Yes; various. (2) Yes.

Reports about the patterns of light come from different places in the world. Are the circles or patterns of light in the whole world the same? (March 2002)

So far, more or less.

Are the patterns of light a new phenomenon comparable to the crop circles? (March 2002)

To us, yes. To the Space Brothers, no, not comparable.

Please could you tell me more about the technical creation of the patterns of light? (1) Are they part of the Science of Light? (2) Have they some similarity with laser technology? (July/August 2005)

(1) No. (2) No.

You have talked about the role of crop circles and energetic nodes around the Earth. Is it accurate to say the patterns of light phenomenon is part of this same preparation for the Technology of Light? In other words, are circles of light urban crop circles? (March 2009)

It is true to say that the circles of light phenomenon is part of the preparation for the Technology of Light. It is an illustration of the Space Brothers' command of light phenomena drawing attention to their presence rather than to the Science of Light. But it is not true to say that they are urban crop circles. They have a completely different function.

What is that function? (March 2009)
If I could tell you that I would not be sitting here. I would have the scientists of the world all sitting at my feet wanting to know what it is. If I did know, there is no way I could impart it to you. The answer is I do not know. But what I do know is this: that if we understood the technology that created the patterns of light phenomena we could rid the world of global warming in a very short space of time.

When the sun shines on the front windows of our flat in Amsterdam (near the Share Nederland/International Information Centre) we see light formations outside – on the buildings opposite, on the road and on the pavement. For a number of years the shape remained unchanged. Then I noticed the windows had gone blank – no shapes at all for a few days. Suddenly the light formations returned – only now a completely different shape. (1) Is this really possible? (2) Do they change pattern from time to time and, if so, (3) why? (November 2006)
(1) Yes, you saw it! (2) Yes. (3) To maintain our interest.

Where I live in Pueblo, Colorado, USA, there are patterns of light on an old building by an alley. They come and go and not too many people ask about them or acknowledge their presence. There is a metaphysical shop near the sighting; they are the people who brought them to my attention. As I was observing them, they disappeared. I'd check on them periodically after that, and they come and go. Does this mean that God is coming and that people should know this, or is it a blessing sent from

193

God? (March 2007)

Not God but His representative, the Lord Maitreya. They are a blessing from Maitreya.

I like reading your website. When it comes to the patterns of light photographs I would like to make a statement.

Whenever there is sun in my city of Bergen, Norway, I see the patterns on the walls between buildings. Never ever when it is overcast. It is the sun that makes them, reflecting the light from one window on to the other side of the street. It is a fact. I believe that it is divine. Everything is divine since it is in its essence created by the creator. But to say that it is Maitreya who creates the light on the wall here in Bergen is taking it too far. (September 2007)

It is indeed the sun that makes possible the reflection. The sun has always been there but this phenomenon is only a relatively recent manifestation. The patterns are the result of the association of the Space Brothers with advice from Maitreya as to where, that is, on which walls, to place the patterns.

What is the Aurora Borealis, the Northern Lights? Are they the outer visible form of energies entering our planet? (September 2007)

They are the light of the etheric envelope of Earth which becomes visible in the northern hemisphere under certain conditions.

(1) Is there less prana and etheric energy in large cities than in the countryside? (2) Is there more prana in certain climates? (September 2007)

(1) No, usually the opposite is the case. That is why large cities grow as chakras (force centres) of the planet. (2) Yes. Generally speaking, in dry, sunny climates.

EDUCATION IN THE NEW AGE

*This article, an interview with Benjamin Creme, by George Catlin, first appeared in **Share International** July/August 1997, and was published in **Maitreya's Mission Volume Three**. It is reprinted here for the convenience of the reader, because the same subject matter is discussed from a slightly different angle.*

Our topic is education in the New Age, so perhaps the best place to begin is with some clarification of exactly what you mean by education. What does that term mean to you?

To me, education is every activity that fits a man, woman, or child for the fullest expression of their potential. Coming into incarnation at a certain stage in development, carrying on from a previous life, we have a given potential in terms of soul expression, intelligence, and physical equipment, whatever that brings into this life. Education is the preparation of a man, woman, or child, on physical, emotional, mental, and spiritual planes, to bring out their potential in any given life.

So you're taking education quite broadly then. Would you say that parents are educators?

In the sense that every child imitates its parents from the word go, then indeed every parent is an educator, for good or ill. If the behaviour of the parent is restrictive, authoritarian, then it is bad education. If the parent surrounds the child with love and patience, and seeks to enhance its expression in any given area, then it is taking an essential part in the education of the child. But most of us pass on to our children what we received from our own parents. Most of us receive, and endow our children with, much harmful 'garbage'. I do not call that education but conditioning.

Outside the home and formal schools, would you see places like the workplace as having a potential for education?

Very much so. In fact, I would see in the education of the future a closer relationship between formal schoolroom situations and the outer workplace and community in general. And I would see, as part of education, a growing need to involve children at a young age in full-blown community activities so that they see themselves from the very beginning as part of a community, wider than the family and different from the school – not to replace the school, but to enhance what the school can bring to life.

Given your mention of the future, and the potential for communities emerging in the child's awareness, maybe this is a good time to get into the question of what the New Age is. Could you explain that?
The New Age is the result of the cyclic activity of certain great cosmic energies that impose themselves on the life of our solar system. As it moves around the heavens, our system comes into direct energetic relationship with each constellation of the zodiac in turn. These constellations embody powerful cosmic energies with particular qualities which dominate the life of the cycle for as long as it lasts – roughly 2,150 years per cycle. We are emerging out of the Piscean experience and entering the new age in which the Aquarian energies, which are very different from those of Pisces, will influence us, and create a new culture and civilization as we respond to them. These energies embody certain great ideas which become our ideals; as we put the ideals into effect, so our culture and civilization grows.

Does one age end at a particular moment and a new age begin?
One ends and one begins, but not at a particular moment. There is a transitional phase of roughly 200-300 years. For example, the energies of Pisces began to recede, as our sun moved away from their sphere of influence, around 1625. The energies of Aquarius began to come in 50 years later, around 1675. Every day since 1675 has seen the energies of Aquarius mounting in

potency. This they will do until they reach a zenith and then there will be a gradual declining as the sun moves away from their influence and enters that of Capricorn. That will take roughly 2,350 years.

To get some perspective on the challenges of education as we move into the Aquarian Age, I wonder if you would say something about the state of human consciousness at the dawn of the Piscean Age 2,000 years ago.

It was dark. We have a very clear example of this. A great man, one of the greatest beings who has ever graced this Earth, namely Jesus, lived, worked and carried out a three-year mission in a little country called Palestine. It is extraordinary that a man who exemplified in himself the quality of Love, and to a degree that had never been shown in a man before, could be sent to his death – crucified.

This happened because there was no education. People were benighted. There were a few individuals – in this case, the priests – who could read and probably write. They were the teachers, the rabbis, who controlled the others. You can multiply that across the world. A few people read and the rest were totally uneducated. They were peasants, shepherds, fishermen, toolmakers, and so on, with no education at all. They simply did as they were told. This relationship had gone on from the earliest times.

In the Atlantean civilizations, which are said to have ended about 95,000 years ago, there were a few people, priests and kings, who could read, were educated. The rest of the people simply obeyed, did what they were told. The Master Djwhal Khul, writing through Alice Bailey, says that a scholar of the Middle Ages had a consciousness equal to that of a 14-year-old child of the present.

In every age, in every century, there have been those individuals who stood out; for instance, among the Greeks,

Aristotle, Pythagoras, Plato, Socrates, Euclid and all the other extraordinary minds who have given us the embryonic beginnings of the science and philosophy of today. But they were the exception. We have to remember, too, that the "glory that was Greece" was built on slave labour.

The exceptions certainly dominate our sense of history, but at the time of Jesus, what was the average person, the man or woman in the street, able to do and think? Can you describe their consciousness in any way?

They could not think. They could certainly be stimulated and made to act in a certain direction. But it was purely an emotional reaction to excitement. It was in no sense thinking for themselves. Otherwise, for example, Jesus would not have been killed. The populace was whipped up by the priests to get rid of Jesus.

Would you say that we can think now?
We are beginning to think.

Is that the result of the energies of Pisces?
The energies of Pisces have brought out humanity's individuality. This is a great step forward in the evolution of the human race. We have come out of the herd; we were really intelligent animals in the human herd. Broadly speaking, people today are individual in a very real sense; quite distinct from what pertained 2,000 years ago. This is the result of the energy of Pisces. Also, the quality of idealism, the aspiration and vision so prevalent today, has been responsible for the growth of the ideologies and religions. People are now ready to die for their beliefs. This would have seemed unthinkable 2,000 years ago. This is an extraordinary, self-sacrificing view of life, visionary, and fundamentally spiritual.

Is it inevitable that we progress in a certain way as a result of the energies of a particular age?

If we handle them correctly then we do progress. Each energy gives to humanity the ability to unfold a further aspect of our potential, divine nature. Individually, we can slip back, of course, but each age confers on humanity, in an upward spiral, the enhancement of the quality of its consciousness. There is not an equal response by all people because we are not all at the same level of evolution. In relation to our point in evolution, so will we respond to these energies, and they will enhance our ability to develop our fuller potential with each age.

Is there choice involved in that? Have we maximized the opportunity of Pisces? Could things have developed differently? Have we done all that we could have achieved through Pisces?

I doubt it. Separativeness, which has also been a result of the energies of Pisces, has hindered the development of humanity and created great negative karma, both personal and racial. We have hindered ourselves tremendously. Separativeness, of course, is the great hindrance to evolution. There is no separation; this is the heresy of heresies. We are souls in incarnation; there is no such thing as a separate soul.

The fundamental need of any new approach to education will be the understanding, the realization as a fact in life, of the soul.

Given that soul realization would be the overall aim of evolution, what particular aspect will Aquarius draw forth? What energies does Aquarius bring?

Above all, the energy of synthesis. You can already see the effect of the energy of synthesis if you look at almost anything in life, certainly education.

Synthesis has to do with relationships – for instance, the relationship of ideas. Through philosophical investigation you can broaden the consciousness until what seemed the most distant can be seen as standing side by side. Not only complementing and completing each other, but throwing light on each other. It is this ability to synthesize that inevitably broadens the consciousness of humanity and makes correct human relationships possible.

These energies of Aquarius, with their synthesizing quality, will broaden the individualistic consciousness until it can embrace the one humanity. So that we can stand fully individual, unique, and at the same time as one part of this great group which we call humanity.

Even in the abstract that sounds like a huge step forward for human consciousness. How do you imagine that playing out in more concrete terms, in terms of institutions and forms of daily living?

This is a difficult one because the forms are not yet there. Experimentation is going on throughout the world, in some countries more than others. It will make for a growing group consciousness. People will see themselves more and more as part of a group.

In educational establishments, in business, in every aspect of life, you will find groups forming. People who want to make their voices heard in the political field, for instance, form, or join, parties. A party is simply a big group. That group can make known its general ideology, beliefs, intentions, hopes and aspirations in a more powerful way than can the individual.

In this way the world gradually becomes more unified because we find that, although people are individual, they all need the same things. Everybody needs enough food, shelter, housing, clothes, healthcare and education. These requirements, which are common to every man, woman and child on the planet, will more and more become the accepted norm. When they are seen to be the basic requirements for all, we will see global consciousness become a fact.

Unfortunately, up until now, education in most countries has been very nationalistic. People have been taught the history of their nation, usually in a very biased form: everything that nation did was good, and everything other nations did was bad. This has given a very jaundiced, and quite incorrect, vision of the world to the developing child.

I would say that education, in the first place, has to show the child that it is a member of a world family. The synthesizing energy of Aquarius must be used to create this global consciousness. Children need to be shown that we are not living alone in one large or small country, but in a world shared by 5.7 billion people. The child, above all, should be taught that this is the fundamental position of his/her life on Earth: that they are one of a group, a family. Just as a family shares the resources that come into the household, so the human family should share the resources that are given by Divine Providence for that purpose.

It is hard for me to see consciousness, individuals, and education moving in that direction. In the face of world need, people seem to be getting ever more individualistic.

We have the expression, today, probably, of the greatest greed that we can imagine, although compared with what one knows about Atlantis, we do not know what greed is. They had the greatest greed that has ever been: rich people who bathed in milk, kings who stored gold by the ton, and some castles which were actually made of gold. Everyone else lived little better than animals: they thought like animals (if you could call it thinking), they emoted like animals, they obeyed like animals. Those above them, the kings and chiefs who could think, completely dominated all life. For most people, life was very brutish.

Today, we have growing wealth and growing greed around the world, as the mechanism for making money becomes more and more refined. The techniques of making money are now so exquisite that people can make a living out of doing just that. At the same time, more and more people are realizing the needs of

201

the one humanity. They realize that millions of people are starving to death, and countless millions more are living in utter poverty, degradation, misery and want. That gap, the discrepancy between the rich and poor, is the real problem.

This cannot go on for ever. There is a growing awareness that things have to change. The very speed of the advance of greed through market forces and competition is forcing us to the edge of a precipice. This will suddenly bring us face to face with reality. There are various portents of breakdown in our economic structure. When such events occur, they will transform the present economic system, probably forever.

You have spent most of your recent life emphasizing that, soon, and potentially shortly after this kind of economic readjustment, the externalization of the Spiritual Hierarchy will complete itself and that the Masters will emerge into public view led by the Christ. How is that going to affect education?

The fundamental purpose of education, as I see it, is to equip people to demonstrate their divine potential as souls in incarnation. The externalization of the work of the Masters will have an enormous physical, emotional, mental, and psychological impact on humanity. We will come to realize that the soul really does exist. They, the Masters, are the Kingdom of Souls. People like Jesus will be talking to the people daily. He is alive and well and, if you can believe me, has been living in Rome for the last seven years. The Master of all the Masters, the Lord Maitreya, has been living in London (although moving around the world at will) since 1977. If these are facts, then the fact of the Hierarchy will also demonstrate the fact of the soul. People will say: "That was Saint John," or "That was Saint Peter." But today He is the Master Koot Hoomi or the Master Morya.

It will become clear that reincarnation is a fact of life. This will transform human thinking about the reason for our being on the Earth. We will come to know the answers to the age-old questions: "Why are we here? Who are we? What is the purpose of life? Where are we going?" It will become clear that we are here for a certain purpose: the evolution of the soul in incarnation, carrying out the evolutionary process.

Every soul comes into incarnation with a given set of purposes. Each person's education should be geared to facilitate that process, the working out of the soul's purpose in life. This means that teachers, the educators, whether in school or out of school, must know the point in evolution of any given child. They must know the focus of their consciousness, what really commands their greatest attention, the polarization, as it is called, of their consciousness. Is it on the physical plane? (I do not think any human being is polarized on the physical plane today.) Is it on the astral, the mental, or the spiritual plane?

With the vast majority of people, it will be found that their polarization, the seat of their consciousness, is the astral/emotional plane. That being so, the point of education for these people will be to lift their consciousness onto the mental plane. If they are mentally polarized, then the educational aim will be the raising of consciousness from the mental to the spiritual level, so that they become spiritually polarized.

How will teachers be able to assess that? Is that something that one can be trained to perceive?
With the Masters working openly in the world, They will train Their disciples. Today we have schoolteachers who are trained to teach children to read, write, do arithmetic, and so on. It is a very limited range of ideas which a teacher is called upon to evoke from the pupil. In most cases it is not even that; it is a limited set of ideas which the teacher is instructed to teach the child by rote to adhere to and accept. That, to my mind, is not education at all.

Education should be the evocation of the potential, whether emotional, mental, or spiritual, of each individual child.

203

Teachers need to be equipped with the new psychology, which is soul psychology. They have to know the point in evolution of the child. They have to know the seat of consciousness, where the child is polarized. And they have to know the governing energies, or rays, of each individual child.

Every individual is governed on all levels – soul, personality, mental, emotional, and physical – by certain rays, streams of energy, seven in number. You can have one of each of these rays or just a few. The personality, mental, astral/emotional and physical rays can change from life to life while the soul ray remains the same for a world cycle, which is an immeasurably long period of time. When these rays are known, the propensities, the lines of greater or lesser resistance for any individual child will be known. This will help the educator to teach the child the best way to proceed to bring out its talents – to go along the line of least resistance when that is the right thing to do, or to tackle a line of greater resistance when that might evoke a trait which is trying hard to express itself and finding it difficult.

It is one thing to understand the rays in the abstract, but it is quite another to be able to assess that in an individual. Will that be the result of specific training that teachers will receive?
Yes. People will have specific training. It is not so very difficult to recognize the rays. If you really study them and make it a daily habit of mind – looking at people and visualizing them in terms of their rays – it is relatively easy for intelligent people who are interested in the subject to become pretty accurate in the delineation of a person's ray structure.

This will move education out of the classroom. When we think of teachers, we usually think of one teacher in the class. I do not see any reason why a much richer kind of education could not be given. Instead of one teacher, they could have a series of teachers from outside who are educators. They might be artists, scientists, esotericists, policemen, doctors, who will give them the benefit of their life experience, which is what students need.

They do not need simply specific teaching, as it is given today, along a subject line only. They need that too, of course. But you can broaden the consciousness of a child. Most children find that what they later think of as their best education came from inspiring parents, uncles, teachers, friends – people who have caught their imagination in life.

If the community really took education seriously, which I am sure it will eventually do, days could be set aside for meetings with philosophers, scientists, and so on, who will donate a day, a week, or whatever, to come into colleges and schools and give the benefit of their experience along their own line of work. In this way the gifts of unusual, and unusually gifted, people can be better put at the service of the growing population.

Earlier you mentioned "lines of least and greater resistance". Could you expand on that a little bit? What is a line of least resistance and why shouldn't one just follow it wherever it leads?

It is sometimes better to do what is hardest for us. That brings out qualities of self-discipline that are very necessary. I am not talking about discipline imposed, but self-discipline, which is probably the most important thing we can do, as long as it is correctly managed. Just to discipline oneself for no reason, as many ascetics do, especially religious ascetics who beat themselves, does nothing but harden the nature and turn one against the world and life.

If your line of least resistance is to be rather lazy, take life easy, not try very hard, it could well be an impediment to progress from the soul's point of view in that life. You may well need to tackle the things you do not like doing, the things that are difficult. If you can do that, discipline yourself in these ways, you can become more disciplined in the bigger ways, the ways that really matter.

I think education is also about the disciplining of the individual in the management of his or her life, and his or her potential, given by the rays. Anybody with a 3rd-ray mind has a very active mind, creative, lively, full of ideas. They could, however, be overactive and manipulative, never learning to sit still, to look inwards and find the meaning of life. Then there are other rays, like the 6th, which is very idealistic and yearning for the higher vision and the higher inner life. People dominated by the 6th ray can be often very impractical on the outer physical plane. The same is true of the 2nd ray, which is very inturned. It finds that the way into the soul is very easy, a line of no resistance. But the way outward, in relation to the outer physical world and all its demands, is something which is often very difficult for the 2nd-ray personality.

If you can discipline yourself and use your qualities intelligently (which is not easy to do) you can strengthen your weak points and modify your strong points so that – although they will still dominate – they need not obliterate the other aspects of yourself. You strengthen the weak points in the beginning in small ways by little disciplines, until they add up to a strong disciplining will. That is education – self-education – in terms of handling your ray structure, which is really handling life.

Inherent in what you just said is the idea that the problems come in two directions, essentially. One is handling life on the outer plane and knowing how to cope with the external world, and the other is this inner movement toward the soul.

This is the crux of the matter. Up until a certain point in evolution, you are either one or the other: either introverted or extroverted in any given life. That is the path of discipleship, in which you are learning to handle these energies that are driving you inward to soul life and also outward to personality life, sequentially. A whole life can be introverted to the soul, or extroverted to the outer world. The individual in each case has an inner unhappiness because he realizes this, but he really cannot do much about it. When a certain balance has been reached, and the person has integrated the physical, emotional, and mental vehicles, he or she becomes initiate. The sign of the initiate is that he/she can go inward, be introverted at will, but also go out and relate perfectly easily to the outer world, at will.

It would seem that our present education is mostly geared toward relating to the outer world. We are primarily taught skills designed to help one fit into society. What about the developments that might come in the future toward the inner side?

Today, most education, for what it is worth, is education for jobs. People are simply fitted to make their living in the outer commercial world under the whip of competition. This will change. Competition has to give way to co-operation. Above all, it is competition, which is based on greed and fear, that holds humanity back in its most important expression of its oneness, its sense of being part of one group. This has to change. When it does, people will realize, and the Masters will exemplify, the fact of the soul. People will realize that they are souls and will turn to the soul. Then the education for the life of the soul, and the psychology of the soul, will become more and more the norm in our educational system.

I do not mean that we will have only religious education. I am not talking about religion at all. The religious path, as seen by the Masters, is only one of many paths to the demonstration of our innate divinity. God does not reside in the religion, although the religion might help you to realize that divinity. Every aspect of life – politics, economics, religion, art, culture, science, education – can be lived in such a way that what we call God can be known and expressed.

The divine becomes a moment-to-moment experience. That is in fact what it is. It is not a man with a beard sitting up in the sky watching that you are not stealing, lying, or cheating. It is inside you; it is your sense of the divine inside that gradually changes you from lying, cheating, and stealing to not doing these things. Not because somebody is telling you that it is bad, but because you instinctively know that that is not the right way to live with your fellow human beings.

Whatever injures or harms another person is intuitively, instinctively, wrong. A change in behaviour comes about by self-observation and self-determination. These things fall away as you become more aware of, and imbued with, the quality of the soul. That will happen on a wider and wider scale as humanity ceases to compete and learns to co-operate – in the family, in the community, nationally and internationally.

In regard to getting to the state of being able to co-operate and beginning to sense the soul and its values and mission, the World Teacher, the Lord Maitreya, has been quoted as saying that without self-esteem nothing can be done. Is this a first step in that direction? Is that something parents, teachers and schools should be thinking about?

Very much so. One of the saddening things about present education is the way children are put down, told that they are wrong, told not to do that, that this is naughty. This inhibition of the child that goes on all the time has nothing to do with naughtiness. The child has no concept of naughtiness. The child has only desires, instincts, and a looking for adventure. If they were allowed to do that without always being told that they are naughty and wrong, they would grow up without these inhibitions, this lack of self-esteem. They would feel loved, feel that their parents really cared about them, had patience for them, were ready to listen to them, speak with them, and so on. That would give an inner confidence which reflects itself in an ability to make the best of any opportunity presented by life.

What holds most people back is a lack of confidence. That is mainly the result of continual nagging by parents, putting the child down. "You're only a child," or "How could you know?" Everything a child says is sneered at and belittled. I do not mean in every family, but in many. Even among otherwise intelligent and educated people you will find the same kind of down-putting, derision of their children.

Children should never, ever, be derided. It is only a convenience for parents to inhibit the child so that they can keep them under moderate control. People are so overworked and tired, their nervous systems so taut, that they cannot bear the presence and demands of their own children. That is a tragedy for them, for the children and for society as a whole.

Self-esteem is a fundamental need in every human being. The lack of it is what drives people to crime, drug taking, all the abuses, even suicide. All of that is a direct result of the inability of many parents to inculcate a sense of love and understanding, to treat them with a warm, patient, readiness to help, to listen and relate to the child, and give them that essential confidence.

It seems at present that most teachers spend about 50 per cent of their time and energy in school trying just to cope with the problem of discipline, trying to keep children within bounds, in some sense. Are you saying that if the child is well-parented, given this love, that won't be such a problem?

Absolutely. My Master has written for *Share International* that it really is not a problem of discipline at all. It is a question of freedom. It is a matter of seeing the validity of the child, the need of the child for self-expression.

Each child, at whatever level it comes into incarnation, comes into the world with its own set of purposes. A main purpose is to learn to live in peace and harmony with the rest of us, all the people with whom he or she comes into relationship. The actual possibility to do this is rare today. You are a very exceptional individual if you come into life in a family, a school situation, a national community, where everything you need to work out your life purposes as a soul is available to you.

We need to recognize that all young people are unique. They are sons of God evolving towards the manifestation of that divinity and son-ship. How many people see an individual child in that way?

Many parents love their child, but you can love a child and not respect it. To say that you really respect its uniqueness and validity at every turn, I think, is a huge claim. Not many people meet that need of the child.

We have the Year of the Child, but that is playing at the game, this giving respect to the child. The very fact that we have the Year of the Child, however, even if it is only a non-active slogan, means that we are beginning to see the validity of the child and the need to respect it.

A child at any point of evolution comes into incarnation with all its past achievements. There is a wonderful child today, aged 11, who paints pictures that are said to be like Picasso, Matisse, or Chagall – obviously a tremendously gifted child. She is Romanian, living in America, and already fantastically successful. This child is allowed to paint. She is a genius, and is allowed to be a genius. And she does it. Instead of going out to play, she paints these great big canvases and covers them with the most interesting and beautiful ideas.

Children should be introduced to all that they need to further their talents. This is to do with respecting the child as a soul. If you respect each child as a soul, and see that they have all of that behind them, give them the scope in which that can come out, marvels of creativity will come forth.

Do you imagine special kinds of schools for special kinds of development?

I see special kinds of education for specially gifted children – not necessarily special schools. It can be in the same school. But there have to be different departments that will accommodate, enhance and develop the gifts of specially gifted children. Otherwise, the race will suffer.

Today, if you are a specially gifted child, usually sooner or later these gifts show themselves, whatever the circumstances. But a tremendous amount of time may be lost in the process. Some demonstrate only a fragment of their potential because it was not noted when the person most needed it. That will mean training teachers at higher and higher levels. As far as education is concerned, it will only be as good as the quality of the teachers. Training of teachers, I would say, is the fundamental first step in all new educational needs.

There's some writing, particularly by the Master DK, about the possibility of schools starting to become focused more on the problem of reaching beyond the mind to the soul. Do you envision that happening?

Yes, absolutely. Obviously, you need to discipline the instincts. You need to enhance and develop the intellect, the mind and the brain. And you need to evoke the intuition. These are higher and higher steps. The more advanced the individual, the more the intuition will play a role. The bridge to it, the antahkarana, which is created by meditation and service, will become known as a definite part of the educational curriculum. You have to build the bridge. Meditation, therefore, at a certain point in the educational system, will have to come in as the way, par excellence, to create the bridge to the soul.

It is interesting that you mention meditation and service. Many schools are already instituting service components of their education. Many colleges have that as part of their requirements for a degree. It is nice to think that is already happening.

Yes. The more the child is related to the community at an early age, the more service will become normal and natural.

In that same vein, are you suggesting that meditation will be taught in our schools or colleges?

Yes. It should never be imposed at an early stage. I do not believe in making young children meditate, but the beginnings of meditation are beneficial. We discussed the problems of discipline. If the children were to start the day by just sitting quietly for five minutes and taking a few deep breaths, just quietly thinking about themselves and maybe what they are going to do for the rest of the day, just letting these breaths quiet them down, you could have a completely different atmosphere in the school.

And then for older children the more technical training in meditation?

Indeed, the beginnings of meditation, or light meditation, in which the concentration is focused. You have to learn to concentrate, to use the mind, and to meditate and build the bridge to the soul. There are times for doing this. I am not going to set down ages because children vary enormously depending on their point in evolution. Those who are more evolved can start at an earlier age than those less evolved.

I have one last topic that you might address: television and its effect on children.

I would say that television has one of the greatest negative effects on children. It is not the fault of the children but of the type of television. I have found that meditators in America, for example, have very little concentration. Their attention span is very limited. I think it is largely due to the breakup of attention from a very early age, through watching commercial television. It is convenient to let you go and get a cup of coffee, or whatever, but it breaks up the attention in the middle of any programme. Your interest is held for a certain point and then suddenly you have a break, which goes on for almost longer than the preceding episode of the programme you were watching. That is terrible for the concentration.

If it is bad for adults, it is also very bad for children. Children's television is no better in that respect. They have their own set of nasty advertisements telling them to get their parents to buy this, that and the other. This is a social thing. It is to do with competition, greed, the wrong economic systems in the world, which will change when co-operation and sharing replace the present competitive system.

Children have to be taught to concentrate. It does not always come naturally. With some it does: the more evolved, of course, can usually concentrate. Yet there are many gifted children who cannot concentrate at all.

Do you imagine television eventually playing a more positive role?

Yes, indeed. Television will become the great teacher in the world, but it will have to change dramatically in its content, its substance. You can imagine television screens in every home, where the children can be taught about history in the real sense – global history, not nationalistic, chauvinistic history, but the history of humankind throughout the ages – and relate themselves to it. The Masters can project onto the television screens a view of life in the far, far distant past, in Atlantean days, and forward into the future, showing visions of what can be. There will be wonderful programmes for children projected onto the screens by the Masters. Television will be the key tool by which Maitreya and the Masters teach humanity.

TRANSMISSION MEDITATION

A BRIEF EXPLANATION

A group meditation providing both a dynamic service to the world and powerful, personal spiritual development.

Transmission Meditation is a group meditation established to better distribute spiritual energies from their Custodians, the Masters of Wisdom, our planetary Spiritual Hierarchy. It is a means of 'stepping down' (transforming) these energies so that they become accessible and useful to the general public. It is the creation, in co-operation with the Hierarchy of Masters, of a vortex or pool of higher energy for the benefit of humanity.

In March 1974, under the direction of his Master, Benjamin Creme formed the first Transmission Meditation group in London. Today there are hundreds of such groups around the world, and new groups are forming all the time.

Transmission Meditation groups provide a link whereby Hierarchy can respond to world need. The prime motive of this work is service, but it also constitutes a powerful mode of personal growth. Many people are searching for ways in which to improve the world; this desire to serve can be strong, but difficult, in our busy lives, to fulfil. Our soul needs a means to serve, but we do not always respond to its call, and so produce disequilibrium and conflict within ourselves. Transmission Meditation provides a unique opportunity for service in a potent and fully scientific way with the minimum expenditure of one's time and energy.

Benjamin Creme holds Transmission Meditation workshops around the world. During the meditation he is overshadowed by Maitreya, the World Teacher, which allows Maitreya to confer great spiritual nourishment on the participants. Many people are inspired to begin Transmission Meditation after attending such a workshop, and many acknowledge having received healing in the process.

[Please refer to *Transmission: A Meditation for the New Age* by Benjamin Creme, Share International Foundation]

BOOKS BY BENJAMIN CREME

The Reappearance of the Christ and the Masters of Wisdom

Creme's first book gives the background and pertinent information concerning the return of Maitreya, the Christ. Putting the most profound event of the last 2,000 years into its correct historical and esoteric context, Creme describes the effect the World Teacher's presence will have on both the world's institutions and the average person. Topics range from the soul and reincarnation to nuclear energy, UFOs, and a new economic order.

1st edition 1979. 2nd edition 2007. ISBN: 978-90-71484-32-2, 288pp.

Messages from Maitreya the Christ

During the years of preparation for His emergence, Maitreya gave 140 messages through Benjamin Creme during public lectures, using mental overshadowing and the telepathic rapport thus set up. The messages inspire readers to spread the news of His reappearance and to work urgently for the rescue of millions suffering from poverty and starvation in a world of plenty. When read aloud, the messages invoke Maitreya's energy and blessing.

1st edition Vol. I 1981, Vol. II 1986. 2nd, combined, edition 1992, reprinted 2001. ISBN 978-90-71484-22-3, 286pp.

Transmission: A Meditation for the New Age

Describes a dynamic process, introduced to the world by Benjamin Creme's Master in 1974. Groups dedicated to world service transmit spiritual energies directed through them by the Masters of our Spiritual Hierarchy. While the prime motive of this work is service, it is also a powerful means of personal growth. Guidelines are given for the formation of transmission groups, along with answers to many questions relating to the work.

1st edition 1983. 5th edition 2006. ISBN 978-90-71484-35-3, 212pp.

A Master Speaks

Articles by Benjamin Creme's Master from the first 22 volumes of Share International magazine, designed to draw attention to the needs of the present and immediate future. Topics include reason and intuition, health and healing, the art of living, human rights, the end of hunger, sharing for peace, the rise of people power, life in the New Age, the role of man, and many more.

1st edition 1985. 3rd expanded edition 2004. ISBN 978-90-71484-29-2, 452pp.

Maitreya's Mission, Volume One

The first of a trilogy of books which further describe the emergence of Maitreya. This volume can be seen as a guidebook for humanity as it travels on its evolutionary journey. A wide range of subjects is covered, such as: the new teachings of the Christ, meditation, karma, life after death, healing, social transformation, initiation, the role of service, and the Seven Rays.

1st edition 1986. 3rd edition 1993, reprinted 2010. ISBN 978-90-71484-08-7, 419pp.

Maitreya's Mission, Volume Two

This volume contains a diverse collection of Maitreya's teachings through His associate, His highly accurate forecasts of world events, descriptions of His miraculous personal appearances, and accounts of related phenomena and signs. It also includes unique interviews with Creme's Master on current affairs. Future-related topics include new forms of government, schools without walls, energy and thought, the coming Technology of Light, and the art of Self-realization.

1st edition 1993, reprinted 2004. ISBN 978-90-71484-11-7, 753pp.

The Ageless Wisdom Teaching

An overview of humanity's spiritual legacy, this book is a concise and easy-to-understand introduction to the Ageless

Wisdom Teaching. It explains the basic tenets of esotericism, including: the source of the Teaching, the origin of man, the Plan of evolution, rebirth and reincarnation, and the Law of Cause and Effect (karma). Also included is an esoteric glossary and a recommended reading list.

1st edition 1996, reprinted 2009. ISBN 978-90-71484-13-1, 79pp.

Maitreya's Mission, Volume Three

Creme presents a compelling vision of the future, with Maitreya and the Masters openly offering Their guidance and inspiration. Coming times will see peace established; sharing the world's resources the norm; maintaining our environment a top priority. Cities of the world will become centers of great beauty. Creme also looks at ten famous artists – among them da Vinci, Michelangelo and Rembrandt – from a spiritual perspective.

1st edition 1997. 2nd edition 2010. ISBN 978-90-71484-45-2, 694pp.

The Great Approach: New Light and Life for Humanity

Addresses the problems of our chaotic world and its gradual change under the influence of Maitreya and the Masters of Wisdom. It covers such topics as sharing, the USA's quandary, ethnic conflicts, crime, environment and pollution, genetic engineering, science and religion, education, health and healing. It predicts amazing scientific discoveries ahead and shows a world free of war where the needs of all are met.

1st edition 2001. ISBN 978-90-71484-23-0, 320pp.

The Art of Co-operation

Deals with the urgent problems of our time and their solution, based on the Ageless Wisdom Teaching. Locked in ancient competition, we are trying to solve problems using out-worn methods, while the answer – co-operation – lies within our grasp. The book points the way to a world of justice, freedom and peace through a growing appreciation of the unity underlying all life.

1st edition 2002. ISBN 978-90-71484-26-1, 235pp.

Maitreya's Teachings: The Laws of Life

Here we are given a taste of the thoughts of a Being of immeasurable stature, to enable us to understand the path of evolution. To some, Maitreya's extraordinary insights into world events will be of major interest, while to others the secrets of Self-realization, the simple description of experienced truth, will be a revelation. To any seeker, His wisdom will provide a simple path stretching to the mountain-top.

1st edition, 2005. ISBN 978-90-71484-31-5, 258pp.

The Art of Living: Living Within the Laws of Life

In Part One, Creme describes the experience of living as a form of art, like painting or music. To reach a high level of expression requires knowledge and application of fundamental principles such as the Law of Cause and Effect and the Law of Rebirth, all described in detail. Parts Two and Three explain how we can emerge from the fog of illusion to become whole and Self-aware.

1st edition 2006. ISBN 978- 90-71484-37-7, 215pp.

The World Teacher for All Humanity

Presents an overview of the return to the everyday world of Maitreya and His group, the Masters of Wisdom; the enormous changes Maitreya's presence has already brought about; and His recommendations for the immediate future. It describes Maitreya as a great spiritual Avatar of immeasurable love, wisdom and power; and also as a friend and brother of humanity, here to lead us into the age of Aquarius.

1st edition, 2007. ISBN 978-90-71484-39-1, 132pp.

The Awakening of Humanity

A companion volume to The World Teacher for All Humanity,

which emphasizes the nature of Maitreya as the Embodiment of Love and Wisdom. While *The Awakening of Humanity* focuses on the day when Maitreya declares Himself openly as World Teacher for the age of Aquarius. It describes the process of Maitreya's emergence, the steps leading to the Day of Declaration, and humanity's anticipated response to this momentous event.

1st edition 2008. ISBN 978-90-71484-41-4, 141pp.

~ ~ ~

Benjamin Creme's books have been translated and published in Dutch, French, German, Japanese and Spanish by groups responding to this message. Some have also been published in Chinese, Croatian, Finnish, Greek, Hebrew, Italian, Portuguese, Romanian, Russian, Slovenian and Swedish. Further translations are planned. Books are available from local booksellers as well as online vendors.

Share-International.org/books
See also 'Other Languages' on this site.

SHARE INTERNATIONAL MAGAZINE
ISSN 0169-1341

A unique magazine featuring each month: up-to-date information about the emergence of Maitreya, the World Teacher; an article from a Master of Wisdom; expansions of the esoteric teachings; Benjamin Creme's answers to a wide variety of topical and esoteric questions; articles by and interviews with people at the forefront of progressive world change; news from UN agencies and reports of positive developments in the transformation of our world.

Share International brings together the two major directions of New Age thinking — the political and the spiritual. It shows the synthesis underlying the political, social, economic and spiritual changes now occurring on a global scale, and seeks to stimulate practical action to rebuild our world along more just and compassionate lines.

Share International covers news, events and comments related to Maitreya's priorities: an adequate supply of the right food, housing and shelter for all, healthcare and education as universal rights, and the maintenance of ecological balance in the world.

Versions of *Share International* are available in Dutch, French, German, Japanese, Romanian, Slovenian and Spanish. For subscription information, contact the appropriate office below.

For North, Central and South America,
Australia, New Zealand and the Philippines
Share International
PO Box 5668, Santa Monica CA 90409 USA

For the UK
Share International
PO Box 3677, London NW5 1RU, UK

For the rest of the world
Share International
PO Box 41877, 1009 DB Amsterdam, Holland

Subscription information and excerpts from the magazine are published online at: **Share-International.org/magazine**

ABOUT THE AUTHOR

Scottish-born painter and esotericist Benjamin Creme has for over 30 years been preparing the world for the most extraordinary event in human history — the return of our spiritual mentors to the everyday world.

Benjamin Creme has appeared on television, radio and in documentary films worldwide and lectures throughout Western and Eastern Europe, the USA, Japan, Australia, New Zealand, Canada and Mexico.

Trained and supervised over many years by his own Master, he began his public work in 1974. In 1982 he announced that the Lord Maitreya, the long-awaited World Teacher, was living in London, ready to present Himself openly when invited by the media to do so. This event is now imminent.

Benjamin Creme continues to carry out his task as messenger of this inspiring news. His books, thirteen at present, have been translated into many languages. He is also the editor of *Share International* magazine, which circulates in over 70 countries. He accepts no money for any of this work.

Benjamin Creme lives in London, is married, and has three children.